Solutions Manual

for use with

Essentials of Investments

Fifth Edition

Zvi Bodie
Boston University

Alex Kane
University of California-San Diego

Alan Marcus
Boston College

Prepared by
Bruce Swensen
Adelphi University – Dept. of Finance

 Irwin

Boston   Burr Ridge, IL   Dubuque, IA   Madison, WI   New York   San Francisco   St. Louis
Bangkok   Bogotá   Caracas   Kuala Lumpur   Lisbon   London   Madrid   Mexico City
Milan   Montreal   New Delhi   Santiago   Seoul   Singapore   Sydney   Taipei   Toronto

Solutions Manual for use with
ESSENTIALS OF INVESTMENTS
Zvi Bodie, Alex Kane, and Alan Marcus

Published by McGraw-Hill/Irwin, an imprint of The McGraw-Hill Companies, Inc., 1221 Avenue of the
Americas, New York, NY 10020. Copyright © 2004, 2001, 1998, 1996, 1992 by The McGraw-Hill
Companies, Inc. All rights reserved.

1 2 3 4 5 6 7 8 9 0 QPD/QPD 0 9 8 7 6 5 4 3

ISBN 0-07-283739-X

www.mhhe.com

Table of Contents

CHAPTER 1: INVESTMENTS: BACKGROUND AND ISSUES

1. a.   Cash is a financial asset because it is the liability of the federal government.

   b.   No. The cash does not directly add to the productive capacity of the economy.

   c.   Yes.

   d.   Society as a whole is worse off, since taxpayers, as a group will make up for the liability.

2. a.   The bank loan is a financial liability for Lanni. (Lanni's IOU is the bank's financial asset). The cash Lanni receives is a financial asset. The new financial asset created is Lanni's promissory note (that is, Lanni's IOU to the bank).

   b.   Lanni transfers financial assets (cash) to the software developers. In return, Lanni gets a real asset, the completed software. No financial assets are created or destroyed; cash is simply transferred from one party to another.

   c.   Lanni gives the real asset (the software) to Microsoft in exchange for a financial asset, 1,500 shares of stock in Microsoft. If Microsoft issues new shares in order to pay Lanni, then this would represent the creation of new financial assets.

   d.   Lanni exchanges one financial asset (1,500 shares of stock) for another ($120,000). Lanni gives a financial asset ($50,000 cash) to the bank and gets back another financial asset (its IOU). The loan is "destroyed" in the transaction, since it is retired when paid off and no longer exists.

3. a.

Assets		Liabilities & Shareholders' equity	
Cash	$ 70,000	Bank loan	$ 50,000
Computers	30,000	Shareholders' equity	50,000
Total	$100,000	Total	$100,000

   Ratio of real to total assets = $30,000/$100,000 = 0.30

   b.

Assets		Liabilities & Shareholders' equity	
Software product*	$ 70,000	Bank loan	$ 50,000
Computers	30,000	Shareholders' equity	50,000
Total	$100,000	Total	$100,000

   *Valued at cost

   Ratio of real to total assets = $100,000/$100,000 = 1.0

c.

	Assets		Liabilities & Shareholders' equity	
Microsoft shares	$120,000	Bank loan		$ 50,000
Computers	30,000	Shareholders' equity		100,000
Total	$150,000	Total		$150,000

Ratio of real to total assets = $30,000/$150,000 = 0.20

Conclusion: when the firm starts up and raises working capital, it will be characterized by a low ratio of real to total assets. When it is in full production, it will have a high ratio of real assets. When the project "shuts down" and the firm sells it off for cash, financial assets once again replace real assets.

4.   Ultimately, it is true that real assets do determine the material well being of an economy. Nevertheless, individuals can benefit when financial engineering creates new products that allow them to manage their portfolios of financial assets more efficiently. Because bundling and unbundling creates financial products with new properties and sensitivities to various sources of risk, it allows investors to hedge particular sources of risk more efficiently.

5.   The ratio is ($628/$17,252) = 0.036 for the financial sector. The ratio is ($9,568/$17,661) = 0.542 for non-financial firms. The difference should be expected mainly because the bulk of the business of financial institutions is to make loans that are financial assets.

6.   a.   Primary-market transaction

b.   Derivative assets.

c.   Investors who wish to hold gold without the complication and cost of physical storage.

7.   a.   A fixed salary means that compensation is (at least in the short run) independent of the firm's success. This salary structure does not tie the manager's immediate compensation to the success of the firm. However, the manager might view this as the safest compensation structure and therefore value it more highly.

b.   A salary that is paid in the form of stock in the firm means that the manager earns the most when the shareholders' wealth is maximized. This structure is therefore most likely to align the interests of managers and shareholders. If stock compensation is overdone, however, the manager might view it as overly risky since the manager's career is already linked to the firm, and this undiversified exposure would be exacerbated with a large stock position in the firm.

c.   Call options on shares of the firm create great incentives for managers to contribute to the firm's success. In some cases, however, stock options can lead to other agency problems. For example, a manager with numerous call options might be tempted to take on a very risky investment project, reasoning that if the project succeeds the payoff will be huge, while if it fails, the losses are limited to the lost value of the options. Shareholders, in contrast, bear the losses as well as the gains on the project, and might be less willing to assume that risk.

8. Even if an individual shareholder could monitor and improve managers' performance, and thereby increase the value of the firm, the payoff would be small, since the ownership share in a large corporation would be very small. For example, if you own $10,000 of GM stock and can increase the value of the firm by 5%, a very ambitious goal, you benefit by only $(0.05 \times \$10,000) = \$500$.

   In contrast, a bank that has a multimillion-dollar loan outstanding to the firm has a big stake in making sure that the firm can repay the loan. It is clearly worthwhile for the bank to spend considerable resources to monitor the firm.

9. Securitization requires access to a large number of potential investors. To attract these investors, the capital market needs:
   (1) a safe system of business laws and low probability of confiscatory taxation/regulation;
   (2) a well-developed investment banking industry;
   (3) a well-developed system of brokerage and financial transactions, and;
   (4) well-developed media, particularly financial reporting.
   These characteristics are found in (indeed make for) a well-developed financial market.

10. Securitization leads to disintermediation; that is, securitization provides a means for market participants to bypass intermediaries. For example, mortgage-backed securities channel funds to the housing market without requiring that banks or thrift institutions make loans from their own portfolios. As securitization progresses, financial intermediaries must increase other activities such as providing short-term liquidity to consumers and small business, and financial services.

11. Financial assets make it easy for large firms to raise the capital needed to finance their investments in real assets. If General Motors, for example, could not issue stocks or bonds to the general public, it would have a far more difficult time raising capital. Contraction of the supply of financial assets would make financing more difficult, thereby increasing the cost of capital. A higher cost of capital means less investment and lower real growth.

12. Mutual funds accept funds from small investors and invest, on behalf of these investors, in the national and international securities markets.

   Pension funds accept funds and then invest, on behalf of current and future retirees, thereby channeling funds from one sector of the economy to another.

   Venture capital firms pool the funds of private investors and invest in start-up firms.

   Banks accept deposits from customers and loan those funds to businesses, or use the funds to buy securities of large corporations.

13. Even if the firm does not need to issue stock in any particular year, the stock market is still important to the financial manager. The stock price provides important information about how the market values the firm's investment projects. For example, if the stock price rises considerably, managers might conclude that the market believes the firm's future prospects are bright. This might be a useful signal to the firm to proceed with an investment such as an expansion of the firm's business.

   In addition, the fact that shares can be traded in the secondary market makes the shares more attractive to investors since investors know that, when they wish to, they will be able to sell their shares. This in turn makes investors more willing to buy shares in a primary offering, and thus improves the terms on which firms can raise money in the equity market.

14. Treasury bills serve a purpose for investors who prefer a low-risk investment. The lower average rate of return compared to stocks is the price investors pay for predictability of investment performance and portfolio value.

15. With a "top-down" investment strategy, you focus on asset allocation or the broad composition of the entire portfolio, which is the major determinant of overall performance. Moreover, top down management is the natural way to establish a portfolio with a level of risk consistent with your risk tolerance. The disadvantage of an *exclusive* emphasis on top down issues is that you may forfeit the potential high returns that could result from identifying and concentrating in undervalued securities or sectors of the market.

   With a "bottom-up" investment strategy, you try to benefit from identifying undervalued securities. The disadvantage is that you tend to overlook the overall composition of your portfolio, which may result in a non-diversified portfolio or a portfolio with a risk level inconsistent with your level of risk tolerance. In addition, this technique tends to require more active management, thus generating more transaction costs. Finally, your analysis may be incorrect, in which case you will have fruitlessly expended effort and money attempting to beat a simple buy-and-hold strategy.

16. You should be skeptical. If the author actually knows how to achieve such returns, one must question why the author would then be so ready to sell the secret to others. Financial markets are very competitive; one of the implications of this fact is that riches do not come easily. High expected returns require bearing some risk, and obvious bargains are few and far between. Odds are, the only one getting rich from the book is its author.

CHAPTER 2: FINANCIAL INSTRUMENTS

1. d.

2. c.

3. a. You would have to pay the asked price of:
        107:27 = 107.84375% of par = $1,078.4375

    b. The coupon rate is $5\frac{5}{8}\%$, implying coupon payments of $56.25 annually or, more precisely, $28.125 semiannually.

    c. Current yield = (Annual coupon income/price) = $56.25/$1078.4375 = 0.0522 = 5.22%

4. Preferred stock is like long-term debt in that it typically promises a fixed payment each year. In this way, it is a perpetuity. Preferred stock is also like long-term debt in that it does not give the holder voting rights in the firm.

    Preferred stock is like equity in that the firm is under no contractual obligation to make the preferred stock dividend payments. Failure to make payments does not set off corporate bankruptcy. With respect to the priority of claims to the assets of the firm in the event of corporate bankruptcy, preferred stock has a higher priority than common equity but a lower priority than bonds.

5. Money market securities are called "cash equivalents" because of their great liquidity. The prices of money market securities are very stable, and they can be converted to cash (i.e., sold) on very short notice and with very low transaction costs.

6. The total before-tax income is $4. After the 70% exclusion, taxable income is:
    (0.30 × $4) = $1.20. Therefore:

    Taxes = (0.30 × $1.20) = $0.36

    After-tax income = ($4 - $0.36) = $3.64

    After-tax rate of return = ($3.64/$40) = 9.1%

7. a. The closing price is $80.36, which is $3.39 lower than yesterday's price. Therefore, yesterday's closing price was: ($80.36 + $3.39) = $83.75

    b. You could buy: ($5,000/$80.36) = 62.22 shares

    c. Your annual dividend income would be 1.4% of $5,000, or $70.

    d. Earnings per share can be derived from the price-earnings (PE) ratio.
        Price/Earnings = 18 and Price = 80.36 so that Earnings = ($80.36/18) = $4.46

8. a. At t = 0, the value of the index is: $(90 + 50 + 100)/3 = 80$

    At t = 1, the value of the index is: $(95 + 45 + 110)/3 = 83.333$

    The rate of return is: $(83.333/80)/ - 1 = 4.167\%$

    b. In the absence of a split, stock C would sell for 110, and the value of the index would be: $(95 + 45 + 110)/3 = 83.333$
    After the split, stock C sells at 55. Therefore, we need to set the divisor (d) such that:

    $$83.333 = (95 + 45 + 55)/d \Rightarrow d = 2.340$$

    c. The rate of return is zero. The index remains unchanged, as it should, since the return on each stock separately equals zero.

9. a. Total market value at t = 0 is: $(9,000 + 10,000 + 20,000) = 39,000$

    Total market value at t = 1 is: $(9,500 + 9,000 + 22,000) = 40,500$

    Rate of return = $(40,500/39,000) - 1 = 3.85\%$

    b. The return on each stock is as follows:

    $r_A = (95/90) - 1 = 0.0556$

    $r_B = (45/50) - 1 = -0.10$

    $r_C = (110/100) - 1 = 0.10$

    The equally-weighted average is: $[0.0556 + (-0.10) + 0.10]/3 = 0.0185 = 1.85\%$

10. The after-tax yield on the corporate bonds is: $[0.09 \times (1 - 0.28)] = 0.0648 = 6.48\%$
Therefore, the municipals must offer at least 6.48% yields.

11. a. The taxable bond. With a zero tax bracket, the after-tax yield for the taxable bond is the same as the before-tax yield (5%), which is greater than the yield on the municipal bond.

    b. The taxable bond. The after-tax yield for the taxable bond is:
    $[0.05 \times (1 - 0.10)] = 4.5\%$

    c. You are indifferent. The after-tax yield for the taxable bond is:
    $[0.05 \times (1 - 0.20)] = 4.0\%$
    The after-tax yield is the same as that of the municipal bond.

    d. The municipal bond offers the higher after-tax yield for investors in tax brackets above 20%.

12. Equation (2.2) shows that the equivalent taxable yield (r) is: $r = r_m/(1-t)$

    a.   4.00%

    b.   4.44%

    c.   5.00%

    d.   5.71%

13.   a.   The higher coupon bond.

    b.   The call with the lower exercise price.

    c.   The put on the lower priced stock.

14.   a.   The December maturity futures price is $278.30 per ounce. If the contract closes at $283 in December, your profit on each contract (for delivery of 100 ounces of gold) will be: ($283 − $278.30) × 100 = $470.

    b.   There are 77,991 contracts outstanding, calling for delivery of 7,799,100 ounces of gold.

15.   a.   Yes. As long as the stock price at expiration exceeds the exercise price, it makes sense to exercise the call. The gross payoff is: ($107 − $105) = $2.
Your profit net of the cost of purchasing the call is: ($2 − $2.60) = −$0.60
The rate of return over the holding period is: (−0.60/2.60) = −0.2308 = −23.08%

    b.   If you had bought a November expiration call with exercise price 100, it would have cost $5.20 and the gross payoff at expiration would be: ($107 − $100) = $7.
The profit net of the cost of the call is: ($7 - $5.60) = $1.80
The rate of return over the holding period is: ($1.80/$5.20) = 0.3462 = 34.62%

    c.   A put with exercise price 105 would expire worthless for any stock price equal to or greater than 105. An investor in such a put would have a rate of return over the holding period of −100%.

16. There is always a chance that the option will expire in the money. Investors will pay something for this chance of a positive payoff.

17.

	Value of call at expiration	Initial Cost	Profit
a.	0	4	-4
b.	0	4	-4
c.	0	4	-4
d.	5	4	1
e.	10	4	6

	Value of put at expiration	Initial Cost	Profit
a.	10	6	4
b.	5	6	-1
c.	0	6	-6
d.	0	6	-6
e.	0	6	-6

18. A put option conveys the *right* to sell the underlying asset at the exercise price. A short position in a futures contract carries an *obligation* to sell the underlying asset at the futures price.

19. A call option conveys the *right* to buy the underlying asset at the exercise price. A long position in a futures contract carries an *obligation* to buy the underlying asset at the futures price.

20. The spread will widen. Deterioration of the economy increases credit risk, that is, the likelihood of default. Investors will demand a greater premium on debt securities subject to default risk.

21. Twenty of the twenty-five stocks meet this criterion, leading us to conclude that prices on individual stocks can be quite volatile.

CHAPTER 3: HOW SECURITIES ARE TRADED

1. a. In addition to the explicit fees of $70,000, FBN appears to have paid an implicit price in underpricing of the IPO. The underpricing is $3 per share, or a total of $300,000, implying total costs of $370,000.

    b. No. The underwriters do not capture the part of the costs corresponding to the underpricing. The underpricing may be a rational marketing strategy. Without it, the underwriters would need to spend more resources in order to place the issue with the public. The underwriters would then need to charge higher explicit fees to the issuing firm. The issuing firm may be just as well off paying the implicit issuance cost represented by the underpricing.

2. a. In principle, potential losses are unbounded, growing directly with increases in the price of IBM.

    b. If the stop-buy order can be filled at $128, the maximum possible loss per share is $8. If the price of IBM shares go above $128, then the stop-buy order would be executed, limiting the losses from the short sale.

3. a. The stock is purchased for (300 × $40) = $12,000. The amount borrowed is $4,000. Therefore, the investor put up equity, or margin, of $8,000.

    b. If the share price falls to $30, then the value of the stock falls to $9,000. By the end of the year, the amount of the loan owed to the broker grows to:
    ($4,000 × 1.08) = $4,320.
    Therefore, the remaining margin in the investor's account is:
    ($9,000 − $4,320) = $4,680.
    The percentage margin is now: ($4,680/$9,000) = 0.52 = 52%.
    Therefore, the investor will not receive a margin call.

    c. The rate of return on the investment over the year is:
    (Ending equity in the account − Initial equity)/Initial equity
         = ($4,680 − $8,000)/$8,000 = −0.415 = −41.5%

4. a. The initial margin was: (0.50 × 1,000 × $40) = $20,000. Old Economy Traders loses ($10 × 1,000) = $10,000 as a result of the increase in the stock price so margin decreases by $10,000. Moreover, Old Economy Traders must pay the dividend of $2 per share to the lender of the shares, so that the margin in the account decreases by an additional $2,000. Therefore, the remaining margin is: ($20,000 - $10,000 - $2,000) = $8,000

    b. The percentage margin is: ($8,000/$50,000) = 0.16 = 16%, so there will be a margin call.

    c. The equity in the account decreased from $20,000 to $8,000 in one year, for a rate of return of: (−$12,000/$20,000) = −0.60 = −60%

5. Much of what the specialist does (e.g., crossing orders and maintaining the limit order book) can be accomplished by a computerized system. In fact, some exchanges use an automated system for night trading. A more difficult issue to resolve is whether the more discretionary activities of specialists involving trading for their own accounts (e.g., maintaining an orderly market) can be replicated by a computer system.

6. a. The buy order will be filled at the best limit-sell order price: $50.25

   b. The next market buy order will be filled at the next-best limit-sell order price: $51.50

   c. You would want to increase your inventory. There is considerable buying demand at prices just below $50, indicating that downside risk is limited. In contrast, limit sell orders are sparse, indicating that a moderate buy order could result in a substantial price increase.

7. a. You buy 200 shares of Telecom for $10,000. These shares increase in value by 10%, or $1,000. You pay interest of: $(0.08 \times 5,000) = \$400$. The rate of return will be:

$$\frac{\$1,000 - \$400}{\$5,000} = 0.12 = 12\%$$

   b. The value of the 200 shares is 200P. Equity is (200P – $5,000). You will receive a margin call when:

$$\frac{200P - \$5,000}{200P} = 0.30 \Rightarrow \text{when } P = \$35.71 \text{ or lower}$$

8. a. Initial margin is 50% of $5,000 or $2,500.

   b. Total assets are $7,500 ($5,000 from the sale of the stock and $2,500 put up for margin). Liabilities are 100P. Therefore, net worth is ($7,500 – 100P). A margin call will be issued when:

$$\frac{\$7,500 - 100P}{100P} = 0.30 \Rightarrow \text{when } P = \$57.69 \text{ or higher}$$

9. The total cost of the purchase is $(\$40 \times 500) = \$20,000$. You borrow $5,000 from your broker, and invest $15,000 of your own funds. Your margin account starts out with net worth of $15,000.

   a. (i) Net worth increases to: $(\$44 \times 500) - \$5,000 = \$17,000$

   Percentage gain = $2,000/$15,000 = 0.1333 = 13.33%

   (ii) With price unchanged, net worth is unchanged.

   Percentage gain = zero

   (iii) Net worth falls to $(\$36 \times 500) - \$5,000 = \$13,000$

   Percentage gain = –$2,000/$15,000 = –0.1333 = –13.33%

The relationship between the percentage change in the price of the stock and the investor's percentage gain is given by:

$$\% \text{ gain} = \% \text{ change in price} \times \frac{\text{Total investment}}{\text{Investor's initial equity}} = \% \text{ change in price} \times 1.333$$

For example, when the stock price rises from $40 to $44, the percentage change in price is 10%, while the percentage gain for the investor is:

$$\% \text{ gain} = 10\% \times \frac{\$20,000}{\$15,000} = 13.33\%$$

b. The value of the 500 shares is 500P. Equity is (500P – $5,000). You will receive a margin call when:

$$\frac{500P - \$5,000}{500P} = 0.25 \Rightarrow \text{when } P = \$13.33 \text{ or lower}$$

c. The value of the 500 shares is 500P. But now you have borrowed $10,000 instead of $5,000. Therefore, equity is (500P – $10,000). You will receive a margin call when:

$$\frac{500P - \$10,000}{500P} = 0.25 \Rightarrow \text{when } P = \$26.67$$

With less equity in the account, you are far more vulnerable to a margin call.

d. By the end of the year, the amount of the loan owed to the broker grows to: ($5,000 × 1.08) = $5,400. The equity in your account is (500P – $5,400). Initial equity was $15,000. Therefore, your rate of return after one year is as follows:

(i) $\dfrac{(500 \times \$44) - \$5,400 - \$15,000}{\$15,000} = 0.1067 = 10.67\%$

(ii) $\dfrac{(500 \times \$40) - \$5,400 - \$15,000}{\$15,000} = -0.0267 = -2.67\%$

(iii) $\dfrac{(500 \times \$36) - \$5,400 - \$15,000}{\$15,000} = -0.1600 = -16.00\%$

The relationship between the percentage change in the price of Intel and the investor's percentage gain is given by:

$$\% \text{ gain} = \left(\% \text{ change in price} \times \frac{\text{Total investment}}{\text{Investor's initial equity}} \right) - \left(8\% \times \frac{\text{Funds borrowed}}{\text{Investor's initial equity}} \right)$$

For example, when the stock price rises from $40 to $44, the percentage change in price is 10%, while the percentage gain for the investor is:

$$\left(10\% \times \frac{\$20,000}{\$15,000} \right) - \left(8\% \times \frac{\$5,000}{\$15,000} \right) = 10.67\%$$

e. The value of the 500 shares is 500P. Equity is (500P – $5,400). You will receive a margin call when:

$$\frac{500P - \$5,400}{500P} = 0.25 \Rightarrow \text{when } P = \$14.40 \text{ or lower}$$

10. a. The gain or loss on the short position is $(-500 \times \Delta P)$. Invested funds are $15,000. Therefore, rate of return = $(-500 \times \Delta P)/15,000$. The rate of return in each of the three scenarios is:

   (i) rate of return = $(-500 \times \$4)/\$15,000 = -0.1333 = -13.33\%$

   (ii) rate of return = $(-500 \times \$0)/\$15,000 = 0\%$

   (iii) rate of return = $[-500 \times (-\$4)]/\$15,000 = +0.1333 = +13.33\%$

   b. Total assets in the margin account are $20,000 (from the sale of the stock) + $15,000 (the initial margin) = $35,000. Liabilities are 500P. A margin call will be issued when:

$$\frac{\$35,000 - 500P}{500P} = 0.25 \Rightarrow \text{when } P = \$56 \text{ or higher}$$

   c. With a $1 dividend, the short position must now pay on the borrowed shares: ($1/share × 500 shares) = $500. Rate of return is now:

   $[(-500 \times \Delta P) - 500]/15,000$

   (i) rate of return = $[(-500 \times 4) - 500]/15,000 = -0.1667 = -16.67\%$

   (ii) rate of return = $[(-500 \times 0) - 500]/15,000 = -0.0333 = -3.33\%$

   (iii) rate of return = $[(-500) \times (-4) - 500]/15,000 = +0.1000 = +10.00\%$

   Total assets are $35,000, and liabilities are (500P + 500). A margin call will be issued when:

$$\frac{35,000 - 500P - 500}{500P} = 0.25 \Rightarrow \text{when } P = \$55.20 \text{ or higher}$$

11. Answers to this problem will vary.

12. The broker is instructed to attempt to sell your Marriott stock as soon as the Marriott stock trades at a bid price of $38 or less. Here, the broker will attempt to execute, but may not be able to sell at $38, since the bid price is now $37.25. The price at which you sell may be more or less than $38 because the stop-loss becomes a market order to sell at current market prices.

13. a. 55.50

     b. 55.25

     c. The trade will not be executed because the bid price is lower than the price specified in the limit sell order.

     d. The trade will not be executed because the asked price is greater than the price specified in the limit buy order.

14. a. In an exchange market, there can be price improvement in the two market orders. Brokers for each of the market orders (i.e., the buy and the sell orders) can agree to execute a trade inside the quoted spread. For example, they can trade at $55.37, thus improving the price for both customers by $0.12 or $0.13 relative to the quoted bid and asked prices. The buyer gets the stock for $0.13 less than the quoted ask price, and the seller receives $0.12 more for the stock than the quoted bid price.

     b. Whereas the limit order to buy at $55.37 would not be executed in a dealer market (since the asked price is $55.50), it could be executed in an exchange market. A broker for another customer with an order to sell at market would view the limit buy order as the best bid price; the two brokers could agree to the trade and bring it to the specialist, who would then execute the trade.

15. The SuperDot system expedites the flow of orders from exchange members to the specialists. It allows members to send computerized orders directly to the floor of the exchange, which allows the nearly simultaneous sale of each stock in a large portfolio. This capability is necessary for program trading.

16. The dealer sets the bid and asked price. Spreads should be higher on inactively traded stocks and lower on actively traded stocks.

17. a. Over short periods of time, the price of an exchange membership generally increases with increases in trading activity. This makes sense because trading commissions depend on trading volume.

     b. The price of an exchange membership has risen far less in percentage terms than trading volume. This suggests that the commissions charged to traders on "typical" trades have fallen over time.

18. The proceeds from the short sale (net of commission) were: ($14 × 100) − $50 = $1,350. A dividend payment of $200 was withdrawn from the account. Covering the short sale at $9 per share cost you (including commission): ($900 + $50) = $950. Therefore, the value of your account is equal to the net profit on the transaction:
($1350 − $200 − $950) = $200

Note that your profit, $200, equals (100 shares × profit per share of $2). Your net proceeds per share was:

$14	selling price of stock
−$ 9	repurchase price of stock
−$ 2	dividend per share
−$ 1	2 trades × $0.50 commission per share
$ 2	

19. (d) The broker will sell, at current market price, after the first transaction at $55 or less.

20. (b)

21. (d)

3-6

CHAPTER 4: MUTUAL FUNDS & OTHER INVESTMENT COMPANIES

1. The unit investment trust should have lower operating expenses. Because the investment trust portfolio is fixed once the trust is established, it does not have to pay portfolio managers to constantly monitor and rebalance the portfolio as perceived needs or opportunities change.

2. The offering price includes a 6% front-end load, or sales commission, meaning that every dollar paid results in only $0.94 going toward purchase of shares. Therefore:

$$\text{Offering price} = \frac{\text{NAV}}{1 - \text{load}} = \frac{\$10.70}{1 - 0.06} = = \$11.38$$

3. NAV = offering price × (1 − load) = $12.30 × 0.95 = $11.69

4.

Stock	Value held by fund
A	$ 7,000,000
B	12,000,000
C	8,000,000
D	15,000,000
Total	$42,000,000

$$\text{Net asset value} = \frac{\$42,000,000 - \$30,000}{4,000,000} = \$10.49$$

5. Value of stocks sold and replaced = $15,000,000

$$\text{Turnover rate} = \frac{\$15,000,000}{\$42,000,000} = 0.357 = 35.7\%$$

6. a. $$\text{NAV} = \frac{\$200\text{million} - \$3\text{million}}{5\text{million}} = \$39.40$$

   b. $$\text{Premium (or discount)} = \frac{\text{Price} - \text{NAV}}{\text{NAV}} = \frac{\$36 - \$39.40}{\$39.40} = -0.086 = -8.6\%$$

   The fund sells at an 8.6% discount from NAV

7. $$\text{Rate of return} = \frac{\Delta \text{NAV} + \text{Distributions}}{\text{Start of year NAV}} = \frac{-\$0.40 + \$1.50}{\$12.50} = 0.0880 = 8.80\%$$

8.   a.   Start of year price = $12.00 \times 1.02 = \$12.24$

End of year price = $12.10 \times 0.93 = \$11.25$

Although NAV increased, the price of the fund fell by $0.99.

$$\text{Rate of return} = \frac{\Delta(\text{Price}) + \text{Distributions}}{\text{Start of year price}} = \frac{-\$0.99 + \$1.50}{\$12.24} = 0.0417 = 4.17\%$$

b.   An investor holding the same portfolio as the fund manager would have earned a rate of return based on the increase in the NAV of the portfolio:

$$\text{Rate of return} = \frac{\Delta(\text{NAV}) + \text{Distributions}}{\text{Start of year NAV}} = \frac{\$0.10 + \$1.50}{\$12.00} = 0.1333 = 13.33\%$$

9.   a.   *Unit investment trusts*: diversification from large-scale investing, lower transaction costs associated with large-scale trading, low management fees, predictable portfolio composition, guaranteed low portfolio turnover rate.

b.   *Open-end funds*: diversification from large-scale investing, lower transaction costs associated with large-scale trading, professional management that may be able to take advantage of buy or sell opportunities as they arise, record keeping.

c.   *Individual stocks and bonds*: No management fee, realization of capital gains or losses can be coordinated with investor's personal tax situation, portfolio can be designed to investor's specific risk profile.

10.   Open-end funds are obligated to redeem investor's shares at net asset value, and thus must keep cash or cash-equivalent securities on hand in order to meet potential redemptions. Closed-end funds do not need the cash reserves because there are no redemptions for closed-end funds. Investors in closed-end funds sell their shares when they wish to cash out.

11.   Balanced funds keep relatively stable proportions of funds invested in each asset class. They are meant as convenient instruments to provide participation in a range of asset classes. Asset allocation funds, in contrast, may vary the proportions invested in each asset class by large amounts as predictions of relative performance across classes vary. Asset allocation funds therefore engage in more aggressive market timing.

12. a.   Empirical research indicates that past performance of mutual funds is not highly predictive of future performance, especially for better-performing funds. While there *may* be some tendency for the fund to be an above average performer next year, it is unlikely to once again be a top 10% performer.

   b.   On the other hand, the evidence is more suggestive of a tendency for poor performance to persist. This tendency is probably related to fund costs and turnover rates. Thus if the fund is among the poorest performers, investors would be concerned that the poor performance will persist.

13.   Start of year NAV = $20

   Dividends per share = $0.20

   End of year NAV is based on the 8% price gain, less the 1% 12b-1 fee:

   End of year NAV = $20 × (1.08) × (1 − 0.01) = $21.384

   $$\text{Rate of return} = \frac{\$21.384 - \$20 + \$0.20}{\$20} = 0.0792 = 7.92\%$$

14.   The excess of purchases over sales must be due to new inflows into the fund. Therefore, $400 million of stock previously held by the fund was replaced by new holdings. So turnover is: ($400/$2,200) = 0.182 = 18.2%

15.   Fees paid to investment managers were (0.007 × $2.2 billion) = $15.4 million. Since the total expense ratio was 1.1% and the management fee was 0.7%, we conclude that 0.4% must be for other expenses. Therefore, other administrative expenses were: (0.004 × $2.2 billion) = $8.8 million

16.   As an initial approximation, your return equals the return on the shares minus the total of the expense ratio and purchase costs: (12% − 1.2% − 4%) = 6.8%
   But the precise return is less than this because the 4% load is paid up front, not at the end of the year.

   To purchase the shares, you would have had to invest: [$20,000/(1 − .04)] = $20,833. The shares increase in value from $20,000 to: [$20,000 × (1.12 − 0.012)] = $22,160. The rate of return is: [(22,160 − 20,833)/20,833] = 6.37%

17. Suppose you have $1000 to invest. The initial investment in Class A shares is $940 net of the front-end load. After 4 years, your portfolio will be worth:

$$\$940 \times (1.10)^4 = \$1,376.25$$

Class B shares allow you to invest the full $1,000, but your investment performance net of 12b-1 fees will be only 9.5%, and you will pay a 1% back-end load fee if you sell after 4 years. Your portfolio value after 4 years will be:

$$\$1000 \times (1.095)^4 = \$1,437.66$$

After paying the back-end load fee, your portfolio value will be:

$$\$1,437.66 \times 0.99 = 1423.28$$

Class B shares are the better choice if your horizon is 4 years.

With a 15-year horizon, the Class A shares will be worth:

$$\$940 \times (1.10)^{15} = \$3926.61$$

For the Class B shares, there is no back-end load in this case since the horizon is greater than 5 years. Therefore, the value of the Class B shares will be:

$$\$1000 \times (1.095)^{15} = \$3901.32$$

At this longer horizon, Class B shares are no longer the better choice. The effect of Class B's 0.5% 12b-1 fees cumulates over time and finally overwhelms the 6% load charged to Class A investors.

18. Suppose that finishing in the top half of all portfolio managers is purely luck, and that the probability of doing so in any year is exactly ½. Then the probability that any particular manager would finish in the top half of the sample five years in a row is $(\frac{1}{2})^5 = 1/32$. We would then expect to find that $[350 \times (1/32)] = 11$ managers finish in the top half for each of the five consecutive years. This is precisely what we found. Thus, we should not conclude that the consistent performance after five years is proof of skill. We would expect to find eleven managers exhibiting precisely this level of "consistency" even if performance is due solely to luck.

19. a. After two years, each dollar invested in a fund with a 4% load and a portfolio return equal to r will grow to: $[\$0.96 \times (1 + r - 0.005)^2]$. Each dollar invested in the bank CD will grow to $[\$1 \times (1.06)^2]$. If the mutual fund is to be the better investment, then the portfolio return, r, must satisfy:

$$0.96 \times (1 + r - 0.005)^2 > (1.06)^2$$

$$0.96 \times (1 + r - 0.005)^2 > 1.1236$$

$$(1 + r - 0.005)^2 > 1.1704$$

$$1 + r - 0.005 > 1.0819$$

$$1 + r > 1.0869$$

Therefore, $r > 0.0869 = 8.69\%$

b.   If you invest for six years, then the portfolio return must satisfy:

$$0.96 \times (1 + r - 0.005)^6 > (1.06)^6 = 1.4185$$

$$(1 + r - 0.005)^6 > 1.4776$$

$$1 + r - 0.005 > 1.0672$$

$$1 + r > 1.0722$$

$$r > 7.22\%$$

The cutoff rate of return is lower for the six year investment because the "fixed cost" (i.e., the one-time front-end load) is spread out over a greater number of years.

c.   With a 12b-1 fee instead of a front-end load, the portfolio must earn a rate of return (r) that satisfies:

$$1 + r - 0.005 - 0.0075 > 1.06$$

In this case, r must exceed 7.25% regardless of the investment horizon.

20.   The turnover rate is 50%. This means that, on average, 50% of the portfolio is sold and replaced with other securities each year. Trading costs on the sell orders are 0.4%; and the buy orders to replace those securities entail another 0.4% in trading costs. Total trading costs will reduce portfolio returns by: $(2 \times 0.4\% \times 0.50) = 0.4\%$

21.   For the bond fund, the fraction of portfolio income given up to fees is:

$$\frac{0.6\%}{4.0\%} = 0.150 = 15.0\%$$

For the equity fund, the fraction of investment earnings given up to fees is:

$$\frac{0.6\%}{12.0\%} = 0.050 = 5.0\%$$

Fees are a much higher fraction of expected earnings for the bond fund, and therefore may be a more important factor in selecting the bond fund.

This may help to explain why unmanaged unit investment trusts are concentrated in the fixed income market. The advantages of unit investment trusts are low turnover and low trading costs and management fees. This is a more important concern to bond-market investors.

CHAPTER 5: RISK AND RETURN: PAST AND PROLOGUE

1. $V(12/31/2000) = V(1/1/1994) \times (1 + g)^7 = 100{,}000 \times (1.05)^7 = \$140{,}710.04$

2. i and ii. The standard deviation is non-negative.

3.   c.   Determines most of the portfolio's return and volatility over time.

4. $E(r) = [0.3 \times 44\%] + [0.4 \times 14\%] + [0.3 \times (-16\%)] = 14\%$

   $\sigma^2 = [0.3 \times (44 - 14)^2] + [0.4 \times (14 - 14)^2] + [0.3 \times (-16 - 14)^2] = 540$

   $\sigma = 23.24\%$

   The mean is unchanged, but the standard deviation has increased.

5.   a.   The holding period returns for the three scenarios are:
   Boom: $(50 - 40 + 2)/40 = 0.30 = 30.00\%$
   Normal: $(43 - 40 + 1)/40 = 0.10 = 10.00\%$
   Recession: $(34 - 40 + 0.50)/40 = -0.1375 = -13.75\%$

   $E(HPR) = [(1/3) \times 30\%] + [(1/3) \times 10\%] + [(1/3) \times (-13.75\%)] = 8.75\%$

   $\sigma^2(HPR) = [(1/3) \times (30 - 8.75)^2] + [(1/3) \times (10 - 8.75)^2] + [(1/3) \times (-13.75 - 8.75)^2]$
         $= 319.79$

   $\sigma = \sqrt{319.79} = 17.88\%$

      b. $E(r) = (0.5 \times 8.75\%) + (0.5 \times 4\%) = 6.375\%.$

   $\sigma = 0.5 \times 17.88\% = 8.94\%$

6.   c.   [For each portfolio: Utility $= E(r) - (0.5 \times 4 \times \sigma^2)$
   We choose the portfolio with the highest utility value.]

7.   d.   [When an investor is risk neutral, A = 0, so that the portfolio with the highest utility is the portfolio with the highest expected return.]

8.   b.

9.   d.

10. c.

11. b.

12. b.   The probability is 0.50 that the state of the economy is neutral. Given a neutral economy, the probability that the performance of the stock will be poor is 0.30, and the probability of both a neutral economy and poor stock performance is: $0.30 \times 0.50 = 0.15$

13. b.

14. a.   Time-weighted average returns are based on year-by-year rates of return.

Year	Return = [(capital gains + dividend)/price]
1999-2000	$(110 - 100 + 4)/100 = 14.00\%$
2000-2001	$(90 - 110 + 4)/110 = -14.55\%$
2001-2002	$(95 - 90 + 4)/90 = 10.00\%$

Arithmetic mean: 3.15%
Geometric mean: 2.33%

b.

Time	Cash flow	Explanation
0	-300	Purchase of three shares at $100 per share
1	-208	Purchase of two shares at $110, plus dividend income on three shares held
2	110	Dividends on five shares, plus sale of one share at $90
3	396	Dividends on four shares, plus sale of four shares at $95 per share

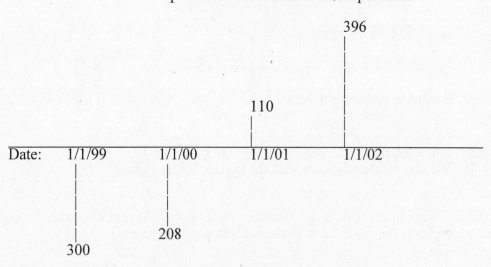

Dollar-weighted return = Internal rate of return = –0.1661%.

15. a. $E(r_p) - r_f = \frac{1}{2}A\sigma_p^2 = \frac{1}{2} \times 4 \times (0.20)^2 = 0.08 = 8.0\%$

   b. $0.09 = \frac{1}{2}A\sigma_p^2 = \frac{1}{2} \times A \times (0.20)^2 \Rightarrow A = 0.09/(\frac{1}{2} \times 0.04) = 4.5$

   c. Increased risk tolerance means decreased risk aversion (A), which results in a decline in risk premiums.

16. For the period 1926 – 2001, the mean annual risk premium for large stocks over T-bills is: (12.49% - 3.85%) = 8.64%

   $E(r)$ = Risk-free rate + Risk premium = 5% + 8.64% = 13.64%

17. In the table below, we use data from Table 5.3 and the approximation: $r \cong R - i$:

   Small Stocks: $r \cong 18.29\% - 3.15\% = 15.14\%$
   Large Stocks: $r \cong 12.49\% - 3.15\% = 9.34\%$
   Long-Term T-Bonds: $r \cong 5.53\% - 3.15\% = 2.38\%$
   Intermediate-Term T-Bonds: $r \cong 5.30\% - 3.15\% = 2.15\%$

   Next, we compute real rates using the exact relationship:

   $$r = \frac{1+R}{1+i} - 1 = \frac{R-i}{1+i} =$$

   Small Stocks: $r = 15.14\%/1.0315 = 14.68\%$
   Large Stocks: $r = 9.34\%/1.0315 = 9.05\%$
   Long-Term T-Bonds: $r = 2.38\%/1.0315 = 2.31\%$
   Intermediate-Term T-Bonds: $r = 2.15\%/1.0315 = 2.08\%$

18. a. The expected cash flow is: $(0.5 \times \$50,000) + (0.5 \times \$150,000) = \$100,000$. With a risk premium of 10%, the required rate of return is 15%. Therefore, if the value of the portfolio is X, then, in order to earn a 15% expected return:

   $X(1.15) = \$100,000 \Rightarrow X = \$86,957$

   b. If the portfolio is purchased at \$86,957, and the expected payoff is \$100,000, then the expected rate of return, $E(r)$, is:

   $$\frac{\$100,000 - \$86,957}{\$86,957} = 0.15 = 15.0\%$$

   The portfolio price is set to equate the expected return with the required rate of return.

   c. If the risk premium over T-bills is now 15%, then the required return is: 5% + 15% = 20%. The value of the portfolio (X) must satisfy:

   $X(1.20) = \$100,000 \Rightarrow X = \$83,333$

   d. For a given expected cash flow, portfolios that command greater risk premia must sell at lower prices. The extra discount from expected value is a penalty for risk.

19. a. $E(r_P) = (0.3 \times 7\%) + (0.7 \times 17\%) = 14\%$ per year

$\sigma_P = 0.7 \times 27\% = 18.9\%$ per year

b.

Security		Investment Proportions
T-Bills		30.0%
Stock A	$0.7 \times 27\% =$	18.9%
Stock B	$0.7 \times 33\% =$	23.1%
Stock C	$0.7 \times 0\% =$	28.0%

c.   Your Reward-to-variability ratio $= S = \dfrac{17-7}{27} = 0.3704$

Client's Reward-to-variability ratio $= \dfrac{14-7}{18.9} = 0.3704$

d.   See following graph.

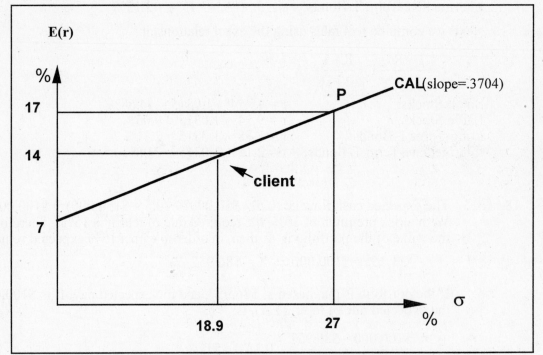

20. a.   Mean of portfolio $= (1 - y)r_f + y\, r_P = r_f + (r_P - r_f)y = 7 + 10y$

If the expected rate of return for the portfolio is 15%, then, solving for y:

$15 = 7 + 10y \Rightarrow y = \dfrac{15-7}{10} = 0.8$

Therefore, in order to achieve an expected rate of return of 15%, the client must invest 80% of total funds in the risky portfolio and 20% in T-bills.

b.

Security		Investment Proportions
T-Bills		20.0%
Stock A	$0.8 \times 27\% =$	21.6%
Stock B	$0.8 \times 33\% =$	26.4%
Stock C	$0.8 \times 40\% =$	32.0%

c. $\sigma_P = 0.8 \times 27\% = 21.6\%$ per year

21. a. Portfolio standard deviation = $\sigma_P = y \times 27\%$

   If the client wants a standard deviation of 20%, then:

   $y = (20\%/27\%) = 0.7407 = 74.07\%$ in the risky portfolio.

   b. Expected rate of return = $7 + 10y = 7 + (0.7407 \times 10) = 7 + 7.407 = 14.407\%$

22. a. Slope of the CML $= \dfrac{13-7}{25} = 0.24$

   See the diagram below.

   b. My fund allows an investor to achieve a higher expected rate of return for any given standard deviation than would a passive strategy, i.e., a higher expected return for any given level of risk.

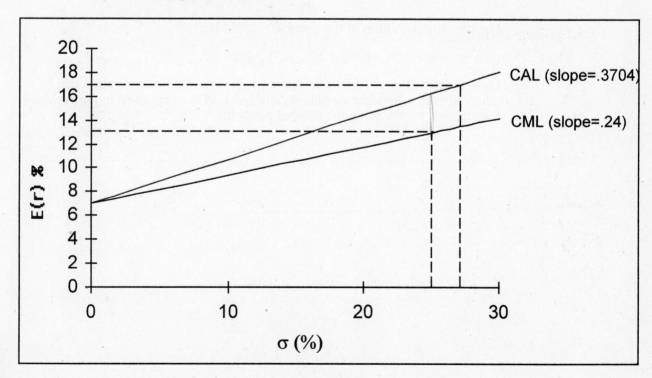

23.   a.   With 70% of his money in my fund's portfolio, the client has an expected rate of return of 14% per year and a standard deviation of 18.9% per year. If he shifts that money to the passive portfolio (which has an expected rate of return of 13% and standard deviation of 25%), his overall expected return and standard deviation would become:

$$E(r_C) = r_f + 0.7(r_M - r_f)$$

In this case, $r_f = 7\%$ and $r_M = 13\%$. Therefore:

$$E(r_C) = 7 + (0.7 \times 6) = 11.2\%$$

The standard deviation of the complete portfolio using the passive portfolio would be:

$$\sigma_C = 0.7 \times \sigma_M = 0.7 \times 25\% = 17.5\%$$

Therefore, the shift entails a decline in the mean from 14% to 11.2% and a decline in the standard deviation from 18.9% to 17.5%. Since both mean return *and* standard deviation fall, it is not yet clear whether the move is beneficial. The disadvantage of the shift is apparent from the fact that, if my client is willing to accept an expected return on his total portfolio of 11.2%, he can achieve that return with a lower standard deviation using my fund portfolio rather than the passive portfolio. To achieve a target mean of 11.2%, we first write the mean of the complete portfolio as a function of the proportions invested in my fund portfolio, y:

$$E(r_C) = 7 + y(17 - 7) = 7 + 10y$$

Because our target is: $E(r_C) = 11.2\%$, the proportion that must be invested in my fund is determined as follows:

$$11.2 = 7 + 10y \Rightarrow y = \frac{11.2 - 7}{10} = 0.42$$

The standard deviation of the portfolio would be:

$$\sigma_C = y \times 27\% = 0.42 \times 27\% = 11.34\%$$

Thus, by using my portfolio, the same 11.2% expected rate of return can be achieved with a standard deviation of only 11.34% as opposed to the standard deviation of 17.5% using the passive portfolio.

b. The fee would reduce the reward-to-variability ratio, i.e., the slope of the CAL. Clients will be indifferent between my fund and the passive portfolio if the slope of the after-fee CAL and the CML are equal. Let f denote the fee:

$$\text{Slope of CAL with fee} = \frac{17-7-f}{27} = \frac{10-f}{27}$$

$$\text{Slope of CML (which requires no fee)} = \frac{13-7}{25} = 0.24$$

Setting these slopes equal and solving for f:

$$\frac{10-f}{27} = 0.24$$

$$10 - f = 27 \times 0.24 = 6.48$$

$$f = 10 - 6.48 = 3.52\% \text{ per year}$$

24. Assuming no change in tastes, that is, an unchanged risk aversion, investors perceiving higher risk will demand a higher risk premium to hold the same portfolio they held before. If we assume that the risk-free rate is unaffected, the increase in the risk premium would require a higher expected rate of return in the equity market.

25. b.

26. c. Expected return for your fund = T-bill rate + risk premium = 6% + 10% = 16%

Expected return of client's overall portfolio = $(0.6 \times 16\%) + (0.4 \times 6\%) = 12\%$

Standard deviation of client's overall portfolio = $0.6 \times 14\% = 8.4\%$

27. a. $\text{Reward to variability ratio} = \dfrac{\text{Risk premium}}{\text{Standard deviation}} = \dfrac{10}{14} = 0.71$

28.

Average Rate of Return, Standard Deviation and Reward-to-Variability Ratio of the Risk Premiums of Small Common Stocks over One Month Bills for 1926-2001 and Various Sub-Periods			
	Risk Premium(%)		Reward-to-
	Mean	SD	Variability Ratio
1926-1944	23.15	61.68	0.3753
1945-1963	15.27	30.01	0.5090
1964-1982	13.46	37.26	0.3612
1983-2001	5.88	20.22	0.2909
1926-2001	14.44	39.98	0.3612

Table 5.5 for comparison			
	Risk Premium(%)		Reward-to-
	Mean	SD	Variability Ratio
1926-1944	8.03	28.69	0.2798
1945-1963	14.41	18.83	0.7655
1964-1982	2.22	17.56	0.1265
1983-2001	9.91	14.77	0.6709
1926-2001	8.64	20.70	0.4176
Source: Data in Table 5.3			

a. For the entire period (1926-2001), small stocks had a lower reward-to-variability ratio (0.3612) than large stocks (0.4176). However, in two of the four sub-periods, small stocks performed better than large stocks.

b. Yes.

29.

Average Real Return, Standard Deviation and Reward-to-Variability Ratio for Large Stocks, 1926-2001 and Various Sub-Periods			
	Risk Premium(%)		Reward-to-
	Mean	SD	Variability Ratio
1926-1944	8.69	27.50	0.3161
1945-1963	13.13	19.94	0.6587
1964-1982	2.75	16.91	0.1629
1983-2001	12.34	14.85	0.8312
1926-2001	9.23	20.38	0.4529

Except for the period 1945-1963, reward-to-variability ratios for real rates are higher than those for excess returns.

30.

Average Real Return, Standard Deviation and Reward-to-Variability Ratio for Small Stocks, 1926-2001 and Various Sub-Periods			
	Risk Premium(%)		Reward-to-Variability Ratio
	Mean	SD	
1926-1944	23.44	59.41	0.3945
1945-1963	14.04	30.41	0.4617
1964-1982	13.44	35.58	0.3778
1983-2001	8.46	19.45	0.4352
1926-2001	14.85	38.64	0.3842

Reward-to-variability ratios for real rates show the same relationship between large and small stocks as with excess returns. This suggests that both portfolios have similar correlations with inflation.

CHAPTER 6: EFFICIENT DIVERSIFICATION

1. $E(r_p) = (0.5 \times 15) + (0.4 \times 10) + (0.10 \times 6) = 12.1\%$

2.   a.   –1.0

3.   c.   i and iii only.

4.   a.   The mean return should be equal to the value computed in the spreadsheet. The fund's return is 3% lower in a recession, but 3% higher in a boom. However, the variance of returns should be higher, reflecting the greater dispersion of outcomes in the three scenarios.

   b.   Calculation of mean return and variance for the stock fund:

(A) Scenario	(B) Probability	(C) Rate of Return	(D) Col. B × Col. C	(E) Deviation from Expected Return	(F) Squared Deviation	(G) Col. B × Col. G
Recession	0.3	-14	-4.2	-24.0	576	172.8
Normal	0.4	13	5.2	3.0	9	3.6
Boom	0.3	30	9.0	20.0	400	120.0
	Expected Return =		10.0		Variance =	296.4
					Standard Deviation =	17.22

   c.   Calculation of covariance:

(A) Scenario	(B) Probability	(C) Deviation from Mean Return Stock Fund	(D) Deviation from Mean Return Bond Fund	(E) Col. C × Col. D	(F) Col. B × Col. E
Recession	0.3	-24	10	-240.0	-72
Normal	0.4	3	0	0.0	0
Boom	0.3	20	-10	-200.0	-60
				Covariance =	-132

Covariance has increased because the stock returns are more extreme in the recession and boom periods. This makes the tendency for stock returns to be poor when bond returns are good (and vice versa) even more dramatic.

5. a. One would expect variance to increase because the probabilities of the extreme outcomes are now higher.

    b. Calculation of mean return and variance for the stock fund:

(A)	(B)	(C)	(D)	(E)	(F)	(G)
		Rate of	Col. B × Col. C	Deviation from	Squared	Col. B × Col. G
Scenario	Probability	Return		Expected Return	Deviation	
Recession	0.4	-11	-4.4	-20.0	400	160.0
Normal	0.2	13	2.6	4.0	16	3.2
Boom	0.4	27	10.8	18.0	324	129.6
	Expected Return =		9.0		Variance =	292.8
					Standard Deviation =	17.11

    c. Calculation of covariance:

(A)	(B)	(C)	(D)	(E)	(F)
		Deviation from Mean Return		Col. C × Col. D	Col. B × Col. E
Scenario	Probability	Stock Fund	Bond Fund		
Recession	0.4	-20	10	-200.0	-80
Normal	0.2	4	0	0.0	0
Boom	0.4	18	-10	-180.0	-72
				Covariance =	-152

Covariance has increased because the probabilities of the more extreme returns in the recession and boom periods are now higher. This makes the tendency for stock returns to be poor when bond returns are good (and vice versa) more dramatic.

6. The parameters of the opportunity set are:

$E(r_S) = 15\%$, $E(r_B) = 9\%$, $\sigma_S = 32\%$, $\sigma_B = 23\%$, $\rho = 0.15$, $r_f = 5.5\%$

From the standard deviations and the correlation coefficient we generate the covariance matrix [note that $Cov(r_S, r_B) = \rho\sigma_S\sigma_B$]:

	Bonds	Stocks
Bonds	529.0	110.4
Stocks	110.4	1024.0

The minimum-variance portfolio proportions are:

$$w_{Min}(S) = \frac{\sigma_B^2 - Cov(r_S, r_B)}{\sigma_S^2 + \sigma_B^2 - 2Cov(r_S, r_B)}$$

$$= \frac{529 - 110.4}{1024 + 529 - (2 \times 110.4)} = 0.3142$$

$w_{Min}(B) = 0.6858$

The mean and standard deviation of the minimum variance portfolio are:

$$E(r_{Min}) = (0.3142 \times 15\%) + (0.6858 \times 9\%) = 10.89\%$$

$$\sigma_{Min} = \left[w_S^2 \sigma_S^2 + w_B^2 \sigma_B^2 + 2w_S w_B Cov(r_S, r_B)\right]^{\frac{1}{2}}$$

$$= [(0.3142^2 \times 1024) + (0.6858^2 \times 529) + (2 \times 0.3142 \times 0.6858 \times 110.4)]^{1/2}$$

$$= 19.94\%$$

% in stocks	% in bonds	Exp. return	Std dev.	
00.00	100.00	9.00	23.00	
20.00	80.00	10.20	20.37	
31.42	**68.58**	**10.89**	**19.94**	minimum variance
40.00	60.00	11.40	20.18	
60.00	40.00	12.60	22.50	
70.75	**29.25**	**13.25**	**24.57**	tangency portfolio
80.00	20.00	13.80	26.68	
100.00	00.00	15.00	32.00	

7.

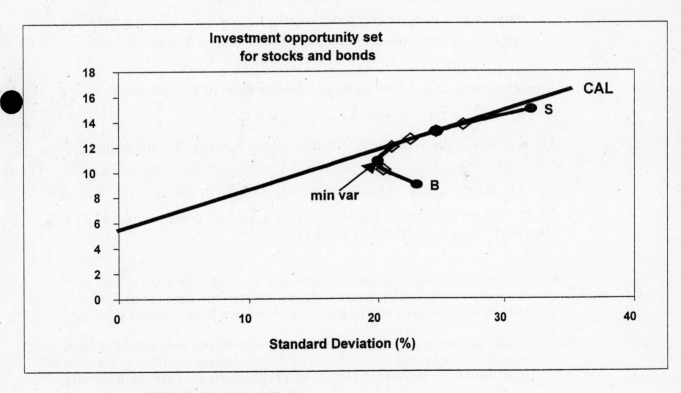

The graph approximates the points:

	E(r)	σ
Minimum Variance Portfolio	10.89%	19.94%
Tangency Portfolio	13.25%	24.57%

8. The reward-to-variability ratio of the optimal CAL is:

$$\frac{E(r_p) - r_f}{\sigma_p} = \frac{13.25 - 5.5}{24.57} = 0.3154$$

9. a. The equation for the CAL is:

$$E(r_C) = r_f + \frac{E(r_p) - r_f}{\sigma_p}\sigma_C = 5.5 + 0.3154\sigma_C$$

Setting $E(r_C)$ equal to 12% yields a standard deviation of 20.61%.

b. The mean of the complete portfolio as a function of the proportion invested in the risky portfolio (y) is:

$$E(r_C) = (1 - y)r_f + yE(r_p) = r_f + y[E(r_p) - r_f] = 5.5 + y(13.25 - 5.5)$$

Setting $E(r_C) = 12\% \Rightarrow y = 0.8387$ (83.87% in the risky portfolio)

$1 - y = 0.1613$ (16.13% in T-bills)

From the composition of the optimal risky portfolio:
Proportion of stocks in complete portfolio = $0.8387 \times 0.7075 = 0.5934$
Proportion of bonds in complete portfolio = $0.8387 \times 0.2925 = 0.2453$

10. Using only the stock and bond funds to achieve a mean of 12% we solve:

$$12 = 15w_S + 9(1 - w_S) = 9 + 6w_S \Rightarrow w_S = 0.5$$

Investing 50% in stocks and 50% in bonds yields a mean of 12% and standard deviation of:

$$\sigma_P = [(0.50^2 \times 1024) + (0.50^2 \times 529) + (2 \times 0.50 \times 0.50 \times 110.4)]^{1/2} = 21.06\%$$

The efficient portfolio with a mean of 12% has a standard deviation of only 20.61%. Using the CAL reduces the SD by 45 basis points.

11. a. Although it appears that gold is dominated by stocks, gold can still be an attractive diversification asset. If the correlation between gold and stocks is sufficiently low, gold will be held as a component in the optimal portfolio.

b. If gold had a perfectly positive correlation with stocks, gold would not be a part of efficient portfolios. The set of risk/return combinations of stocks and gold would plot as a straight line with a negative slope. (See the following graph.) The graph shows that the stock-only portfolio dominates any portfolio containing gold. This cannot be an equilibrium; the price of gold must fall and its expected return must rise.

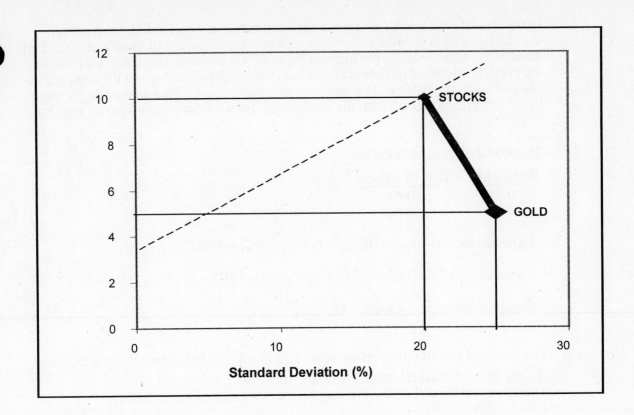

12. Since Stock A and Stock B are perfectly negatively correlated, a risk-free portfolio can be created and the rate of return for this portfolio in equilibrium will always be the risk-free rate. To find the proportions of this portfolio [with w_A invested in Stock A and $w_B = (1 - w_A)$ invested in Stock B], set the standard deviation equal to zero. With perfect negative correlation, the portfolio standard deviation reduces to:

$$\sigma_P = Abs[w_A\sigma_A - w_B\sigma_B]$$

$$0 = 40\,w_A - 60(1 - w_A) \Rightarrow w_A = 0.60$$

The expected rate of return on this risk-free portfolio is:

$$E(r) = (0.60 \times 8\%) + (0.40 \times 13\%) = 10.0\%$$

Therefore, the risk-free rate must also be 10.0%.

13. If the lending and borrowing rates are equal and there are no other constraints on portfolio choice, then optimal risky portfolios of all investors will be identical. However, if the borrowing and lending rates are not equal, then borrowers (who are relatively risk averse) and lenders (who are relatively risk tolerant) will have different optimal risky portfolios.

14 No, it is not possible to get such a diagram. Even if the correlation between A and B were 1.0, the frontier would be a straight line connecting A and B.

15. In the special case that all assets are perfectly positively correlated, the portfolio standard deviation is equal to the weighted average of the component-asset standard deviations. Otherwise, as the formula for portfolio variance (Equation 6.3) shows, the portfolio standard deviation is *less* than the weighted average of the component-asset standard deviations. The portfolio *variance* is a weighted *sum* of the elements in the covariance matrix, with the products of the portfolio proportions as weights.

16. The probability distribution is:

Probability	Rate of Return
0.7	100%
0.3	-50%

Expected return = $(0.7 \times 100\%) + 0.3 \times (-50\%) = 55\%$

Variance = $[0.7 \times (100 - 55)^2] + [0.3 \times (-50 - 55)^2] = 4725$

Standard deviation = $\sqrt{4725} = 68.74\%$

17. The expected rate of return on the stock will change by beta times the unanticipated change in the market return: $1.2 \times (8\% - 10\%) = -2.4\%$
Therefore, the expected rate of return on the stock should be revised to:
$12\% - 2.4\% = 9.6\%$

18. a. The risk of the diversified portfolio consists primarily of systematic risk. Beta measures systematic risk, which is the slope of the SCL. The two figures depict the stocks' security characteristic lines (SCL). Stock B's SCL is steeper, and hence Stock B's systematic risk is greater. The slope of the SCL, and hence the systematic risk, of Stock A is lower. Thus for this investor stock B is the riskiest.

   b. The undiversified investor is exposed primarily to firm-specific risk. Stock A has higher firm-specific risk because the deviations of the observations from the SCL are larger for Stock A than for Stock B. Deviations are measured by the vertical distance of each observation from the SCL. Stock A is therefore riskiest to this investor.

19. A scatter plot results in the following diagram. The slope of the regression line is 2.0 and intercept is 1.0.

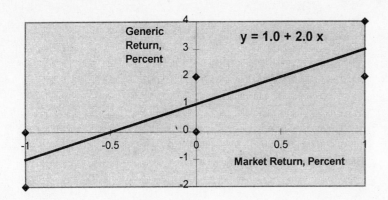

20. a. Restricting the portfolio to 20 stocks, rather than 40 to 50, will very likely increase the risk of the portfolio, due to the reduction in diversification. Such an increase might be acceptable if the expected return is increased sufficiently.

    b. Hennessy could contain the increase in risk by making sure that he maintains reasonable diversification among the 20 stocks that remain in his portfolio. This entails maintaining a low correlation among the remaining stocks. As a practical matter, this means that Hennessy would need to spread his portfolio among many industries, rather than concentrating in just a few.

21. Risk reduction benefits from diversification are not a linear function of the number of issues in the portfolio. (See figure 6.1 in the text.) Rather, the incremental benefits from additional diversification are most important when the portfolio is least diversified. Restricting Hennessy to 10 issues, instead of 20 issues, would increase the risk of his portfolio by a greater amount than reducing the size of the portfolio from 30 to 20 stocks.

22. The point is well taken because the committee should be concerned with the volatility of the entire portfolio. Since Hennessy's portfolio is only one of six well-diversified portfolios, and is smaller than the average, the concentration in fewer issues might have a minimal effect on the diversification of the total fund. Hence, unleashing Hennessy to do stock picking may be advantageous.

23. In the regression of the excess return of Stock ABC on the market, the square of the correlation coefficient is 0.296, which indicates that 29.6% of the variance of the excess return of ABC is explained by the market (systematic risk).

CHAPTER 7: CAPITAL ASSET PRICING
AND ARBITRAGE PRICING THEORY

1. a, c and d.

2. b.

3. $E(r_P) = r_f + \beta[E(r_M) - r_f]$

    $20\% = 5\% + \beta(15\% - 5\%) \Rightarrow \beta = 15/10 = 1.5$

4. If the beta of the security doubles, then so will its risk premium. The current risk premium for the stock is: $(13\% - 7\%) = 6\%$, so the new risk premium would be 12%, and the new discount rate for the security would be: $12\% + 7\% = 19\%$

    If the stock pays a constant dividend in perpetuity, then we know from the original data that the dividend, D, must satisfy the equation for a perpetuity:

    Price = Dividend/Discount rate

    $40 = D/0.13 \Rightarrow D = 40 \times 0.13 = \$5.20$

    At the new discount rate of 19%, the stock would be worth: $(\$5.20/0.19) = \$27.37$
    The increase in stock risk has lowered the value of the stock by 31.58%.

5. The cash flows for the project comprise a 10-year annuity of $10 million per year plus an additional payment in the tenth year of $10 million (so that the total payment in the tenth year is $20 million). The appropriate discount rate for the project is:

    $r_f + \beta[E(r_M) - r_f] = 9\% + 1.7(19\% - 9\%) = 26\%$

    Using this discount rate:

    $$NPV = -20 + \sum_{t=1}^{10} \frac{10}{1.26^t} + \frac{10}{1.26^{10}}$$

    $= -20 + [10 \times \text{Annuity factor } (26\%, 10 \text{ years})] + [10 \times \text{PV factor } (26\%, 10 \text{ years})]$

    $= 15.64$

    The internal rate of return on the project is 49.55%. The highest value that beta can take before the hurdle rate exceeds the IRR is determined by:

    $49.55\% = 9\% + \beta(19\% - 9\%) \Rightarrow \beta = 40.55/10 = 4.055$

6.   a.   False. $\beta = 0$ implies $E(r) = r_f$, not zero.

   b.   False. Investors require a risk premium for bearing systematic (i.e., undiversifiable or market) risk.

   c.   False. You should invest 0.75 of your portfolio in the market portfolio, and the remainder in T-bills. Then:

$$\beta_{P} = (0.75 \times 1) + (0.25 \times 0) = 0.75$$

7.   a.   The beta is the sensitivity of the stock's return to the market return. Call A the aggressive stock and D the defensive stock. Then beta is the change in the stock return per unit change in the market return. Therefore, we compute each stock's beta by calculating the difference in its return across the two scenarios divided by the difference in market return.

$$\beta_A = \frac{2 - 32}{5 - 20} = 2.00$$

$$\beta_D = \frac{3.5 - 14}{5 - 20} = 0.70$$

   b.   With the two scenarios equal likely, the expected rate of return is an average of the two possible outcomes:

$$E(r_A) = 0.5 \times (2\% + 32\%) = 17\%$$

$$E(r_B) = 0.5 \times (3.5\% + 14\%) = 8.75\%$$

   c.   The SML is determined by the following: T-bill rate = 8% with a beta equal to zero, beta for the market is 1.0, and the expected rate of return for the market is:

$$0.5 \times (20\% + 5\%) = 12.5\%$$

See the following graph.

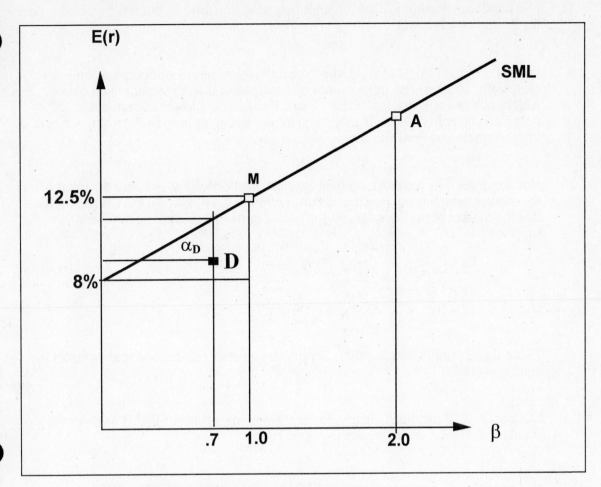

The equation for the security market line is:

$$E(r) = 8\% + \beta(12.5\% - 8\%)$$

d.   The aggressive stock has a fair expected rate of return of:

$$E(r_A) = 8\% + 2.0(12.5\% - 8\%) = 17\%$$

The security analyst's estimate of the expected rate of return is also 17%. Thus the alpha for the aggressive stock is zero. Similarly, the required return for the defensive stock is:

$$E(r_D) = 8\% + 0.7(12.5\% - 8\%) = 11.15\%$$

The security analyst's estimate of the expected return for D is only 8.75%, and hence:

α_D = actual expected return − required return predicted by CAPM

= 8.75% − 11.15% = −2.4%

The points for each stock are plotted on the graph above.

e.   The hurdle rate is determined by the project beta (i.e., 0.7), not by the firm's beta. The correct discount rate is therefore 11.15%, the fair rate of return on stock D.

8.   Not possible. Portfolio A has a higher beta than Portfolio B, but the expected return for Portfolio A is lower.

9.   Possible. If the CAPM is valid, the expected rate of return compensates only for systematic (market) risk as measured by beta, rather than the standard deviation, which includes nonsystematic risk. Thus, Portfolio A's lower expected rate of return can be paired with a higher standard deviation, as long as Portfolio A's beta is lower than that of Portfolio B.

10.   Not possible. The reward-to-variability ratio for Portfolio A is better than that of the market, which is not possible according to the CAPM, since the CAPM predicts that the market portfolio is the most efficient portfolio. Using the numbers supplied:

$$S_A = \frac{16-10}{12} = 0.5$$

$$S_M = \frac{18-10}{24} = 0.33$$

These figures imply that Portfolio A provides a better risk-reward tradeoff than the market portfolio.

11.   Not possible. Portfolio A clearly dominates the market portfolio. It has a lower standard deviation with a higher expected return.

12.   Not possible. Given these data, the SML is: $E(r) = 10\% + \beta(18\% - 10\%)$

A portfolio with beta of 1.5 should have an expected return of:

$$E(r) = 10\% + 1.5 \times (18\% - 10\%) = 22\%$$

The expected return for Portfolio A is 16% so that Portfolio A plots below the SML (i.e., has an alpha of –6%), and hence is an overpriced portfolio. This is inconsistent with the CAPM.

13.   Not possible. The SML is the same as in Problem 12. Here, the required expected return for Portfolio A is: $(10\% + 0.9 \times 8\%) = 17.2\%$, which is still higher than 16%. Portfolio A is overpriced, with alpha equal to –1.2%.

14.   Possible. Portfolio A's ratio of risk premium to standard deviation is less attractive than the market's. This situation is consistent with the CAPM. The market portfolio should provide the highest reward-to-variability ratio.

15. Since the stock's beta is equal to 1, its expected rate of return should be equal to that of the market, that is, 18%.

$$E(r) = \frac{D + P_1 - P_0}{P_0}$$

$$0.18 = \frac{9 + P_1 - 100}{100} \Rightarrow P_1 = \$109$$

16. If beta is zero, the cash flow should be discounted at the risk-free rate, 8%:

PV = $1,000/0.08 = $12,500

If, however, beta is actually equal to 1, the investment should yield 18%, and the price paid for the firm should be:

PV = $1,000/0.18 = $5,555.56

The difference, $6944.44, is the amount you will overpay if you erroneously assume that beta is zero rather than 1.

17. Using the SML: $6\% = 8\% + \beta(18\% - 8\%) \Rightarrow \beta = -2/10 = -0.2$

18. $r_1 = 19\%$; $r_2 = 16\%$; $\beta_1 = 1.5$; $\beta_2 = 1$

   a. In order to determine which investor was a better selector of individual stocks we look at the abnormal return, which is the ex-post alpha; that is, the abnormal return is the difference between the actual return and that predicted by the SML. Without information about the parameters of this equation (i.e., the risk-free rate and the market rate of return) we cannot determine which investment adviser is the better selector of individual stocks.

   b. If $r_f = 6\%$ and $r_M = 14\%$, then (using alpha for the abnormal return):

   $$\alpha_1 = 19\% - [6\% + 1.5(14\% - 6\%)] = 19\% - 18\% = 1\%$$

   $$\alpha_2 = 16\% - [6\% + 1.0(14\% - 6\%)] = 16\% - 14\% = 2\%$$

   Here, the second investment adviser has the larger abnormal return and thus appears to be the better selector of individual stocks. By making better predictions, the second adviser appears to have tilted his portfolio toward under-priced stocks.

   c. If $r_f = 3\%$ and $r_M = 15\%$, then:

   $$\alpha_1 = 19\% - [3\% + 1.5(15\% - 3\%)] = 19\% - 21\% = -2\%$$

   $$\alpha_2 = 16\% - [3\% + 1.0(15\% - 3\%)] = 16\% - 15\% = 1\%$$

   Here, not only does the second investment adviser appear to be a better stock selector, but the first adviser's selections appear valueless (or worse).

19.   a.   Since the market portfolio, by definition, has a beta of 1, its expected rate of return is 12%.

     b. $\beta = 0$ means the stock has no systematic risk. Hence, the portfolio's expected rate of return is the risk-free rate, 5%.

     c.   Using the SML, the *fair* rate of return for a stock with $\beta = -0.5$ is:

$$E(r) = 5\% + (-0.5)(12\% - 5\%) = 1.5\%$$

The *expected* rate of return, using the expected price and dividend for next year:

$$E(r) = (\$44/\$40) - 1 = 0.10 = 10\%$$

Because the expected return exceeds the fair return, the stock must be under-priced.

20.   The data can be summarized as follows:

	Expected Return	Beta	Standard Deviation
Portfolio A	11%	0.8	10%
Portfolio B	14%	1.5	31%
S & P 500	12%	1.0	20%
T-bills	6%	0.0	0%

     a.   Using the SML, the expected rate of return for any portfolio P is:

$$E(r_P) = r_f + \beta[E(r_M) - r_f]$$

Substituting for portfolios A and B:

$$E(r_A) = 6\% + 0.8 \times (12\% - 6\%) = 10.8\%$$

$$E(r_B) = 6\% + 1.5 \times (12\% - 6\%) = 15.0\%$$

Hence, Portfolio A is desirable and Portfolio B is not.

     b.   The slope of the CAL supported by a portfolio P is given by:

$$S = \frac{E(r_P) - r_f}{\sigma_P}$$

Computing this slope for each of the three alternative portfolios, we have:

     S (S&P 500) = 6/20

     S (A) = 5/10

     S (B) = 8/31

Hence, portfolio A would be a good substitute for the S&P 500.

21. Since the beta for Portfolio F is zero, the expected return for portfolio F equals the risk-free rate. For Portfolio A, the ratio of risk premium to beta is: $(10\% - 4\%)/1 = 6\%$. The ratio for Portfolio E is higher: $(9\% - 4\%)/(2/3) = 7.5\%$. This implies that an arbitrage opportunity exists. For instance, you can create a Portfolio G with beta equal to 1 (the same as the beta for Portfolio A) by taking a long position in Portfolio E and a short position in Portfolio F (that is, borrowing at the risk-free rate and investing the proceeds in Portfolio E). For the beta of G to equal 1, the proportion, w, of funds invested in E must be $3/2 = 1.5$. The expected return of G is then:

$$E(r_G) = [(-0.50) \times 4\%] + (1.5 \times 9\%) = 11.5\%$$

$$\beta_G = 1.5 \times (2/3) = 1.0$$

Comparing Portfolio G to Portfolio A, G has the same beta and a higher expected return. Now, consider Portfolio H, which is a short position in Portfolio A with the proceeds invested in Portfolio G:

$$\beta_H = 1\beta_G + (-1)\beta_A = (1 \times 1) + [(-1) \times 1] = 0$$

$$E(r_H) = (1 \times r_G) + [(-1) \times r_A] = (1 \times 11.5\%) + [(-1) \times 10\%] = 1.5\%$$

The result is a zero investment portfolio (all proceeds from the short sale of Portfolio A are invested in Portfolio G) with zero risk (because $\beta = 0$ and the portfolios are well diversified), and a positive return of 1.5%. Portfolio H is an arbitrage portfolio.

22. a. As a first step, convert the scenario rates of return to dollar payoffs per share, as shown in the table below:

	Price	Scenarios 1	2	3
A	$10	$10(1 - 0.15) = \$ 8.50$	$10(1 + 0.20) = \$12.00$	$10(1 + 0.30) = \$13.00$
B	$15	$15(1 + 0.25) = \$18.75$	$15(1 + 0.10) = \$16.50$	$15(1 - 0.10) = \$13.50$
C	$50	$50(1 + 0.12) = \$56.00$	$50(1 + 0.15) = \$57.50$	$50(1 + 0.12) = \$56.00$

Identifying an arbitrage opportunity always involves a zero investment portfolio. This portfolio must show non-negative payoffs in all scenarios. For example, the proceeds from selling short two shares of A *and* two shares of B will be sufficient to buy one share of C.

$$[(-2) \times 10] + [(-2) \times 15] + 50 = 0$$

The payoff table for this zero investment portfolio for all scenarios is:

	Price	# of shares	Investment	Scenarios 1	Scenarios 2	Scenarios 3
A	$10	-2	-$20	-17.0	-24.0	-26.0
B	$15	-2	-$30	-37.5	-33.0	-27.0
C	$50	+1	$50	56.0	57.5	56.0
			$0	+1.5	+0.5	+3.0

This portfolio qualifies as an arbitrage portfolio because it is a zero investment portfolio and it has positive returns in all scenarios.

b. Should the prices of Stock A and Stock B decrease due to excess short selling while the price of Stock C increases because of buying pressures, then the rate of return on $(A + B)$ will increase and the rate of return on Stock C will decrease.

A program that checks for the elimination of *all* arbitrage opportunities will constrain the portfolio proportion so that total invested equals zero. It will then require that the *best* scenario for any such portfolio will have a positive payoff while the *worst* scenario for any such portfolio will have a negative payoff.

We now find a price change that is guaranteed to eliminate the arbitrage opportunity shown above. First note that, as the price of C changes, so will the proportion in any zero investment portfolio. Second, the weakest scenario for a portfolio long on C and short on $(A + B)$ appears to be scenario 2. Keeping the number of shares of A and B sold short equal, we solve for a zero payoff in scenario 2. Denote by X the number of shares of A and B sold short, and let the proceeds of the short sales be sufficient to long one share of C. Now we set the payoff in scenario 2 to zero:

$$12X + 16.5X + 57.5 = 0 \Rightarrow X = -2.0175$$

This means that we short 2.0175 shares of A and 2.0175 shares of B for each share of C held long. (Note that in the previous arbitrage portfolio X = –2.)

Next, with these shares of A and B sold short, we ask: What is the price of a share of C (P_C) that would bring the portfolio investment to zero?

$$10X + 15X + P_C = 0$$

Substituting X = –2.0175 we get:

$$10(-2.0175) + 15(-2.0175) + P_C = 0 \Rightarrow P_C = 50.4375$$

This means that the minimum price change that is needed to eliminate the arbitrage opportunity is greater than 43.75 cents.

To check our results, let's look at the following payoff table for a price change of 50 cents, that is: $P_C = \$50.50$

	Price	# of shares	Investment	Scenarios 1	Scenarios 2	Scenarios 3
A	$10.00	-2.2	-$20.2	-17.170	-24.24	-26.26
B	$15.00	-2.2	-$30.3	-37.875	-33.33	-27.27
C	$50.50	+1.0	$50.5	56.000	57.50	56.00
			$0	+0.955	-0.07	+2.47

Note that the zero investment portfolio must be recalculated ($X = -2.02$) and that the payoffs are no longer positive in all scenarios (the payoff is negative for scenario 2). Thus the arbitrage opportunity has been eliminated. This exercise proves that the price increase for C eliminates the arbitrage opportunity we found in part (a) (i.e., the arbitrage that uses short sales of an equal number of shares of A and B). However, this change does not eliminate *all* arbitrage opportunities. For example, with $P_C = \$50.50$ an arbitrage portfolio can be formed as follows: $X_A = -1.95$ and $X_B = -2.07$ (representing the number of shares of A and B, respectively, sold short).

23. Substituting the portfolio returns and betas in the expected return-beta relationship, we obtain two equations in the unknowns, the risk-free rate (r_f) and the factor risk premium (F):

$$14.0\% = r_f + 1 \times (F - r_f)$$

$$14.8\% = r_f + 1.1 \times (F - r_f)$$

From the first equation we find that F = 14%. Substituting this value for F into the second equation, we get:

$$14.8\% = r_f + 1.1 \times (14\% - r_f) \Rightarrow r_f = 6\%$$

24. a. Shorting equal amounts of the 10 negative-alpha stocks and investing the proceeds equally in the 10 positive-alpha stocks eliminates the market exposure and creates a zero-investment portfolio. Using equation 7.5, and denoting the market factor as R_M, the expected dollar return is [noting that the expectation of residual risk (e) in equation 7.5 is zero]:

$$\$1,000,000 \times [0.03 + (1.0 \times R_M)] - \$1,000,000 \times [(-0.03) + (1.0 \times R_M)]$$

$$= \$1,000,000 \times 0.06 = \$60,000$$

The sensitivity of the payoff of this portfolio to the market factor is zero because the exposures of the positive alpha and negative alpha stocks cancel out. (Notice that the terms involving R_M sum to zero.) Thus, the systematic component of total risk also is zero. The variance of the analyst's profit is not zero, however, since this portfolio is not well diversified.

For n = 20 stocks (i.e., long 10 stocks and short 10 stocks) the investor will have a $100,000 position (either long or short) in each stock. Net market exposure is zero, but firm-specific risk has not been fully diversified. The variance of dollar returns from the positions in the 20 firms is:

$$20 \times [(100,000 \times 0.30)^2] = 18,000,000,000$$

The standard deviation of dollar returns is $134,164.

b.   If n = 50 stocks (i.e., 25 long and 25 short), $40,000 is placed in each position, and the variance of dollar returns is:

$$50 \times [(40,000 \times 0.30)^2] = 7,200,000,000$$

The standard deviation of dollar returns is $84,853.

Similarly, if n = 100 stocks (i.e., 50 long and 50 short), $20,000 is placed in each position, and the variance of dollar returns is:

$$100 \times [(20,000 \times 0.30)^2] = 3,600,000,000$$

The standard deviation of dollar returns is $60,000.

Notice that when the number of stocks increases by a factor of 5 (from 20 to 100), standard deviation falls by a factor of $\sqrt{5} = 2.236$, from $134,164 to $60,000.

25.   Any pattern of returns can be "explained" if we are free to choose an indefinitely large number of explanatory factors. If a theory of asset pricing is to have value, it must explain returns using a reasonably limited number of explanatory variables (i.e., systematic factors).

26.   The APT factors must correlate with major sources of uncertainty, i.e., sources of uncertainty that are of concern to many investors. Researchers should investigate factors that correlate with uncertainty in consumption and investment opportunities. GDP, the inflation rate and interest rates are among the factors that can be expected to determine risk premiums. In particular, industrial production (IP) is a good indicator of changes in the business cycle. Thus, IP is a candidate for a factor that is highly correlated with uncertainties related to investment and consumption opportunities in the economy.

27.   The revised estimate of the expected rate of return of the stock would be the old estimate plus the sum of the unexpected changes in the factors times the sensitivity coefficients, as follows:

Revised estimate = 14% + [(1 × 1) + (0.4 × 1)] = 15.4%

28. Equation 7.8 applies here:

$$E(r_P) = r_f + \beta_{P1}[E(r_1) - r_f] + \beta_{P2}[E(r_2) - r_f]$$

We need to find the risk premium for these two factors:

$\gamma_1 = [E(r_1) - r_f]$ and

$\gamma_2 = [E(r_2) - r_f]$

To find these values, we solve the following two equations with two unknowns:

$$40\% = 7\% + 1.8\gamma_1 + 2.1\gamma_2$$

$$10\% = 7\% + 2.0\gamma_1 + (-0.5)\gamma_2$$

The solutions are: $\gamma_1 = 4.47\%$ and $\gamma_2 = 11.86\%$
Thus, the expected return-beta relationship is:

$$E(r_P) = 7\% + 4.47\beta_{P1} + 11.86\beta_{P2}$$

29. a.

30. d.   From the CAPM, the fair expected return = 8% + 1.25 (15% - 8%) = 16.75%
    Actually expected return = 17%
    $\alpha_1 = 17\% - 16.75\% = 0.25\%$

31.

32.

33.

34.   the risk-free rate.]

35. d.   [You need to know the risk-free rate.]

36. Under the CAPM, the only risk that investors are compensated for bearing is the risk that cannot be diversified away (i.e., systematic risk). Because systematic risk (measured by beta) is equal to 1.0 for each of the two portfolios, an investor would expect the same rate of return from each portfolio. Moreover, since both portfolios are well diversified, it does not matter whether the specific risk of the individual securities is high or low. The firm-specific risk has been diversified away from both portfolios.

37. b.

38. c.

39. d.

40. d.

41. c. Investors will take on as large a position as possible only if the mispricing opportunity is an arbitrage. Otherwise, considerations of risk and diversification will limit the position they attempt to take in the mispriced security.

42. d.

43. d.

CHAPTER 8: THE EFFICIENT MARKET HYPOTHESIS

1. The assumptions consistent with efficient markets are (a) and (c). Many independent, profit-maximizing participants [statement (a)] leads to efficient markets. Statement (c) is the result of efficient markets.

2. The correlation coefficient should be zero. If it were not zero, then one could use returns from one period to predict returns in later periods and therefore earn abnormal profits.

3. c. This is a predictable pattern in returns, which should not occur if the stock market is weakly efficient.

4. c. This is a classic filter rule, which would appear to contradict the weak form of the efficient market hypothesis.

5. b. This is the definition of an efficient market.

6. d.

7. c. The P/E ratio is public information so this observation would provide evidence against the semistrong form of the efficient market theory.

8. No, this is not a violation of the EMH. Intel's continuing large profits do not imply that stock market investors who purchased Intel shares after its success already was evident would have earned a high return on their investments.

9. No, this is not a violation of the EMH. This empirical tendency does not provide investors with a tool that will enable them to earn abnormal returns; in other words, it does not suggest that investors are failing to use all available information. An investor could not use this phenomenon to choose undervalued stocks today. The phenomenon instead reflects the fact that stock splits occur as a response to good performance (i.e., positive abnormal returns) which drives up the stock price above a desired "trading range" and then leads managers to split the stock. After the fact, the stocks that happen to have performed the best will be split candidates, but this does not imply that you can identify the best performers early enough to earn abnormal returns.

10. While positive beta stocks respond well to favorable new information about the economy's progress through the business cycle, these should not show abnormal returns around already anticipated events. If a recovery, for example, is already anticipated, the actual recovery is not news. The stock price should already reflect the coming recovery.

11.   Expected rates of return differ because of differential risk premiums.

12.   The market responds positively to *new* news. If the eventual recovery is anticipated, then the recovery is already reflected in stock prices. Only a better-than-expected recovery should affect stock prices.

13.   Over the long haul, there is an expected upward drift in stock prices based on their fair expected rates of return. The fair expected return over any single day is very small (e.g., 12% per year is only about 0.03% per day), so that on any day the price is virtually equally likely to rise or fall. However, over longer periods, the small expected daily returns cumulate, and upward moves are indeed more likely than downward ones.

14.   You should buy the stock. In your view, the firm's management is not as bad as everyone else believes it to be. Therefore, you view the firm as undervalued by the market. You are less pessimistic about the firm's prospects than the beliefs built into the stock price.

15.   Assumptions supporting passive management are:
      a. informational efficiency
      b. primacy of diversification motives

      Active management is supported by the opposite assumptions, in particular, that pockets of market inefficiency exist.

16.   a.   The grandson is recommending taking advantage of (i) the small firm in January anomaly and (ii) the weekend anomaly.

      b.   (i) Concentration of one's portfolio in stocks having very similar attributes may expose the portfolio to more risk than is desirable. The strategy limits the potential for diversification.

           (ii) Even if the study results are correct as described, each such study covers a specific time period. There is no assurance that future time periods would yield similar results.

           (iii) After the results of the studies became publicly known, investment decisions might nullify these relationships. If these firms in fact offered investment bargains, their prices may be bid up to reflect the now-known opportunity.

17. a. Consistent. Half of all managers should outperform the market based on pure luck in any year.

b. Violation. This would be the basis for an "easy money" rule: simply invest with last year's best managers.

c. Consistent. Predictable *volatility* does not convey a means to earn abnormal returns.

d. Violation. The abnormal performance ought to occur in January, when the increased earnings are announced.

e. Violation. Reversals offer a means to earn easy money: simply buy last week's losers.

18. Implicit in the dollar-cost averaging strategy is the notion that stock prices fluctuate around a "normal" level. Otherwise, there is no meaning to statements such as: "when the price is high." How do we know, for example, whether a price of $25 today will be viewed as high or low compared to the stock price in six months from now?

19. No, it is not more attractive as a possible purchase. Any value associated with dividend predictability is already reflected in the stock price.

20. The market may have anticipated even greater earnings. *Compared to prior expectations,* the announcement was a disappointment.

21. The P/E effect and the small-size effect could be used to enhance portfolio performance *if* one could expect these phenomena to persist in the future. However, concentration in these stocks would lead to departures from efficient diversification. In this case, beta would no longer be an adequate descriptor of portfolio risk because non-systematic risk would remain in the portfolio.

22. Reasons to avoid the strategy:
a. You might believe that these effects would no longer persist now that they are widely known.
b. You might decide that too much diversification must be sacrificed in order to exploit these effects.
c. The level of risk resulting from a low P/E, small capitalization emphasis might be inappropriate.
d. You might decide that these "effects" are in fact a reward for bearing risk of a nature not fully captured by the beta of the stock. In other words, it may be that the abnormal returns on these strategies would not appear so high if we could more accurately risk-adjust performance.

23. a. The earnings (and dividend) growth rates of growth stocks may be consistently overestimated by investors. Investors may extrapolate recent earnings (and dividend) growth too far into the future and thereby downplay the inevitable slowdown. At any given time, growth stocks are likely to revert to (lower) mean returns and value stocks are likely to revert to (higher) mean returns, often over an extended future time horizon.

   b. In efficient markets, the current prices of stocks already reflect all known, relevant information. In this situation, growth stocks and value stocks provide the same risk-adjusted expected return.

CHAPTER 9: BOND PRICES AND YIELDS

1. a. Effective annual rate on three-month T-bill:

$$\left(\frac{100{,}000}{97{,}645}\right)^4 - 1 = (1.02412)^4 - 1 = 0.1000 = 10.00\%$$

b. Effective annual interest rate on coupon bond paying 5% semiannually:

$$(1.05)^2 - 1 = 0.1025 = 10.25\%$$

Therefore, the coupon bond has the higher effective annual interest rate.

2. The effective annual yield on the semiannual coupon bonds is 8.16%. If the annual coupon bonds are to sell at par they must offer the same yield, which requires an annual coupon of 8.16%.

3. The bond callable at 105 should sell at a lower price because the call provision is more valuable to the firm. Therefore, its yield to maturity should be higher.

4. The bond price will be lower. As time passes, the bond price, which is now above par value, will approach par.

5. True. Under the expectations hypothesis, there are no risk premia built into bond prices. The only reason for long-term yields to exceed short-term yields is an expectation of higher short-term rates in the future.

6. c. A "fallen angel" is a bond that has fallen from investment grade to junk bond status.

7. Uncertain. Lower inflation usually leads to lower nominal interest rates. Nevertheless, if the liquidity premium is sufficiently great, long-term yields can exceed short-term yields despite expectations of falling short rates.

8. If the yield curve is upward sloping, you cannot conclude that investors expect short-term interest rates to rise because the rising slope could be due to either expectations of future increases in rates or the demand of investors for a risk premium on long-term bonds. In fact the yield curve can be upward sloping even in the absence of expectations of future increases in rates.

9. a. The bond pays $50 every six months.

Current price:

[$50 × Annuity factor(4%, 6)] + [$1000 × PV factor(4%, 6)] = $1,052.42

Assuming the market interest rate remains 4% per half year, price six months from now:

[$50 × Annuity factor(4%, 5)] + [$1000 × PV factor(4%, 5)] = $1,044.52

b. Rate of return =

$$\frac{\$50 + (\$1,044.52 - \$1,052.42)}{\$1,052.42} = \frac{\$50 - \$7.90}{\$1,052.42} = 0.0400 = 4.00\% \text{ per six months}$$

10. a. Use the following inputs: n = 40, FV = 1000, PV = –950, PMT = 40. You will find that the yield to maturity on a semi-annual basis is 4.26%. This implies a bond equivalent yield to maturity of: (4.26% × 2) = 8.52%

Effective annual yield to maturity = $(1.0426)^2 - 1 = 0.0870 = 8.70\%$

b. Since the bond is selling at par, the yield to maturity on a semi-annual basis is the same as the semi-annual coupon, 4%. The bond equivalent yield to maturity is 8%.

Effective annual yield to maturity = $(1.04)^2 - 1 = 0.0816 = 8.16\%$

c. Keeping other inputs unchanged but setting PV = –1050, we find a bond equivalent yield to maturity of 7.52%, or 3.76% on a semi-annual basis.

Effective annual yield to maturity = $(1.0376)^2 - 1 = 0.0766 = 7.66\%$

11. Since the bond payments are now made annually instead of semi-annually, the bond equivalent yield to maturity is same as the effective annual yield to maturity. The inputs are: n = 20, FV = 1000, PV = –price, PMT = 80. The resulting yields for the three bonds are:

Bond Price	Bond equivalent yield = Effective annual yield
$ 950	8.53%
$1000	8.00%
$1050	7.51%

The yields computed in this case are lower than the yields calculated with semi-annual coupon payments. All else equal, bonds with annual payments are less attractive to investors because more time elapses before payments are received. If the bond price is the same with annual payments, then the bond's yield to maturity is lower.

12.

Time	Inflation in year just ended	Par value	Coupon payment	Principal repayment
0		$1,000.00		
1	2%	$1,020.00	$40.80	0
2	3%	$1,050.60	$42.02	0
3	1%	$1,061.11	$42.44	$1,061.11

$$\text{Nominal return} = \frac{\text{Interest} + \text{Price appreciation}}{\text{Initial price}}$$

$$\text{Real return} = \frac{1 + \text{Nominal return}}{1 + \text{Inflation}} - 1$$

	Second year	Third year
Nominal return =	$\dfrac{\$42.02 + \$30.60}{\$1020} = 0.071196$	$\dfrac{\$42.44 + \$10.51}{\$1050.60} = 0.050400$
Real return =	$\dfrac{1.071196}{1.03} - 1 = 0.0400 = 4.00\%$	$\dfrac{1.05040}{1.01} - 1 = 0.0400 = 4.00\%$

The real rate of return in each year is precisely the 4% real yield on the bond.

13. Remember that the convention is to use semi-annual periods:

Price	Maturity (years)	Maturity (half-years)	Semi-annual YTM	Bond equivalent YTM
$400.00	20.00	40.00	2.317%	4.634%
$500.00	20.00	40.00	1.748%	3.496%
$500.00	10.00	20.00	3.526%	7.052%
$376.89	10.00	20.00	5.000%	10.000%
$456.39	10.00	20.00	4.000%	8.000%
$400.00	11.68	23.36	4.000%	8.000%

14.

		Zero	8% coupon	10% coupon
a.	Current prices	$463.19	$1000	$1134.20
b.	Price one year from now	$500.25	$1000	$1124.94
	Price increase	$ 37.06	$ 0.00	-$ 9.26
	Coupon income	$ 0.00	$80.00	$ 100.00
	Income	$ 37.06	$80.00	$ 90.74
	Rate of Return	8.00%	8.00%	8.00%

15. The *reported* bond price is: 100 2/32 percent of par = $1,000.625
However, 15 days have passed since the last semiannual coupon was paid, so accrued interest equals: $[\$35 \times (15/182)] = \$2.885$
The invoice price is the reported price plus accrued interest: $1003.51

16. If the yield to maturity is greater than current yield, then the bond offers the prospect of price appreciation as it approaches its maturity date. Therefore, the bond is selling below par value.

17. The coupon rate is below 9%. If coupon divided by price equals 9%, and price is less than par, then price divided by par is less than 9%.

18. a. The maturity of each bond is 10 years, and we assume that coupons are paid semiannually. Since both bonds are selling at par value, the current yield to maturity for each bond is equal to its coupon rate.

    If the yield declines by 1% to 5% (2.5% semiannual yield), the Sentinal bond will increase in value to 107.79 [n=20; i = 2.5%; FV = 100; PMT = 3]

    The price of the Colina bond will increase, but only to the call price of 102. The present value of *scheduled* payments is greater than 102, but the call price puts a ceiling on the actual bond price.

    b. If rates are expected to fall, the Sentinal bond is more attractive: since it is not subject to being called, its potential capital gains are higher.

    If rates are expected to rise, Colina is a better investment. Its higher coupon (which presumably is compensation to investors for the call feature of the bond) will provide a higher rate of return than the Sentinal bond.

    c. An increase in the volatility of rates increases the value of the firm's option to call back the Colina bond. [If rates go down, the firm can call the bond, which puts a cap on possible capital gains. So higher volatility makes the option to call back the bond more valuable to the issuer.] This makes the Colina bond less attractive to the investor.

19. The price schedule is as follows:

Year	Remaining Maturity (T)	Constant yield value $1000/(1.08)^T$	Imputed interest (Increase in constant yield value)
0 (now)	20 years	$214.55	
1	19	231.71	$17.16
2	18	250.25	18.54
19	1	925.93	
20	0	1000.00	74.07

20. The bond is issued at a price of $800. Therefore, its yield to maturity is 6.8245%. Using the constant yield method, we can compute that its price in one year (when maturity falls to 9 years) will be (at an unchanged yield) $814.60, representing an increase of $14.60. Total taxable income is: ($40 + $14.60) = $54.60

21. a.   Initial price, $P_0 = 705.46$ [n = 20; PMT = 50; FV = 1000; i = 8]

Next year's price, $P_1 = 793.29$ [n = 19; PMT = 50; FV = 1000; i = 7]

$$HPR = \frac{\$50 + (\$793.29 - \$705.46)}{\$705.46} = 0.1954 = 19.54\%$$

b.   Using OID tax rules, the cost basis and imputed interest under the constant yield method are obtained by discounting bond payments at the *original* 8% yield to maturity, and simply reducing maturity by one year at a time:

Constant yield prices: compare these to actual prices to compute capital gains

$P_0 = \$705.46$

$P_1 = \$711.89$ implies implicit interest over first year = $6.43

$P_2 = \$718.84$ implies implicit interest over second year = $6.95

Tax on explicit plus implicit interest in first year

$$= [0.40 \times (\$50 + \$6.43)] = \$22.57$$

Capital gain in first year = Actual price at 7% YTM – constant yield price

$$= \$793.29 - \$711.89 = \$81.40$$

Tax on capital gain = $(0.30 \times \$81.40) = \$24.42$

Total taxes = $22.57 + $24.42 = $46.99

c.   After tax HPR $= \dfrac{\$50 + (\$793.29 - \$705.46) - \$46.99}{\$705.46} = 0.1288 = 12.88\%$

d.   Value of bond after two years equals $798.82 [using n = 18; i = 7]

Total income from the two coupons, including reinvestment income:

$$(\$50 \times 1.03) + \$50 = \$101.50$$

Total funds after two years: ($798.82 + $101.50) = $900.32

Therefore, the $705.46 investment grows to $900.32 after two years.

$$705.46 \times (1 + r)^2 = 900.32 \Rightarrow r = 0.1297 = 12.97\%$$

e.
Coupon received in first year:	$50.00
Tax on coupon @ 40%	– 20.00
Tax on imputed interest ($0.40 \times \$6.43$)	– 2.57
Net cash flow in first year	$27.43

If you invest the year-1 cash flow at an after-tax rate of:

[3% × (1 – 0.40)] = 1.8%, then, by year 2, it will grow to:

($27.43 × 1.018) = $27.92

You sell the bond in the second year for: $798.82

Tax on *imputed* interest in second year: − 2.78   [0.40 × $6.95]

Coupon received in second year, net of tax: + 30.00   [$50 × (1 − 0.40)]

Capital gains tax on sales price: − 23.99   [0.30 × ($798.82 − $718.84)]
   using constant yield value

CF from first year's coupon (reinvested):   + 27.92   [from above]
     TOTAL $829.97

Thus, after two years, the initial investment of $705.46 grows to $829.97:

$$705.46 \times (1+r)^2 = 829.97 \Rightarrow r = 0.0847 = 8.47\%$$

22.   a.   The bond sells for $1,124.72 based on the 3.5% yield to *maturity*:

      [n = 60; i = 3.5; FV = 1000; PMT = 40]

      Therefore, yield to *call* is 3.368% semiannually, 6.736% annually:

      [n = 10; PV = 1124.72 ; FV = 1100; PMT = 40]

   b.   If the call price were $1050, we would set FV = 1050 and redo part (a) to find that yield to call is 2.976% semi-annually, 5.952% annually. With a lower call price, the yield to call is lower.

   c.   Yield to call is 3.031% semiannually, 6.062% annually:

      [n = 4; PV = 1124.72 ; FV = 1100; PMT = 40]

23.   The stated yield to maturity equals 16.075%:
   [n = 10; PV = 900; FV = 1000; PMT = 140]

   Based on *expected* coupon payments of $70 annually, the expected yield to maturity is 8.526%.

24.   The bond is selling at par value. Its yield to maturity equals the coupon rate, 10%. If the first-year coupon is reinvested at an interest rate of r percent, then total proceeds at the end of the second year will be: [100 × (1 + r) + 1100]. Therefore, realized compound yield to maturity will be a function of r as given in the following table:

r	Total proceeds	Realized YTM = $\sqrt{\text{Proceeds}/1000} - 1$
8%	$1208	$\sqrt{1208/1000} - 1 = 0.0991 = 9.91\%$
10%	$1210	$\sqrt{1210/1000} - 1 = 0.1000 = 10.00\%$
12%	$1212	$\sqrt{1212/1000} - 1 = 0.1009 = 10.09\%$

25.   Zero coupon bonds provide no coupons to be reinvested. Therefore, the final value of the investor's proceeds from the bond is independent of the rate at which coupons could be reinvested (if they were paid). There is no reinvestment rate uncertainty with zeros.

26. April 15 is midway through the semi-annual coupon period. Therefore, the invoice price will be higher than the stated ask price by an amount equal to one-half of the semiannual coupon. The ask price is 101.125 percent of par, so the invoice price is:

$$\$1,011.25 + (1/2 \times \$50) = \$1,036.25$$

27. Factors that might make the ABC debt more attractive to investors, therefore justifying a lower coupon rate and yield to maturity, are:
   i.   The ABC debt is a larger issue and therefore may sell with greater liquidity.
   ii. An option to extend the term from 10 years to 20 years is favorable if interest rates ten years from now are lower than today's interest rates. In contrast, if interest rates are rising, the investor can present the bond for payment and reinvest the money for better returns.
   iii. In the event of trouble, the ABC debt is a more senior claim. It has more underlying security in the form of a first claim against real property.
   iv. The call feature on the XYZ bonds makes the ABC bonds relatively more attractive since ABC bonds cannot be called from the investor.
   v.   The XYZ bond has a sinking fund requiring XYZ to retire part of the issue each year. Since most sinking funds give the firm the option to retire this amount at the lower of par or market value, the sinking fund can work to the detriment of bondholders.

28. a. The floating rate note pays a coupon that adjusts to market levels. Therefore, it will not experience dramatic price changes as market yields fluctuate. The fixed rate note therefore will have a greater price range.

   b. Floating rate notes may not sell at par for any of the several reasons:

   The yield spread between one-year Treasury bills and other money market instruments of comparable maturity could be wider than it was when the bond was issued.

   The credit standing of the firm may have eroded relative to Treasury securities that have no credit risk. Therefore, the 2% premium would become insufficient to sustain the issue at par.

   The coupon increases are implemented with a lag, i.e., once every year. During a period of rising interest rates, even this brief lag will be reflected in the price of the security.

   c. The risk of call is low. Because the bond will almost surely not sell for much above par value (given its adjustable coupon rate), it is unlikely that the bond will ever be called.

   d. The fixed-rate note currently sells at only 88% of the call price, so that yield to maturity is above the coupon rate. Call risk is currently low, since yields would have to fall substantially for the firm to use its option to call the bond.

   e. The 9% coupon notes currently have a remaining maturity of fifteen years and sell at a yield to maturity of 9.9%. This is the coupon rate that would be needed for a newly issued fifteen-year maturity bond to sell at par.

f. Because the floating rate note pays a *variable stream* of interest payments to maturity, its yield-to-maturity is not a well-defined concept. The cash flows one might want to use to calculate yield to maturity are not yet known. The effective maturity for comparing interest rate risk of floating rate debt securities with other debt securities is better thought of as the next coupon reset date rather than the final maturity date. Therefore, "yield-to-recoupon date" is a more meaningful measure of return.

29. a. (1) Current yield = Coupon/Price = 70/960 = 0.0729 = 7.29%

(2) YTM = 3.993% semiannually or 7.986% annual bond equivalent yield

[n = 10; PV = (-)960; FV = 1000; PMT = 35]

Then compute the interest rate.

(3) Realized compound yield is 4.166% (semiannually), or 8.332% annual bond equivalent yield. To obtain this value, first calculate the future value of reinvested coupons. There will be six payments of $35 each, reinvested semiannually at a per period rate of 3%:
[PV = 0; PMT = $35; n = 6; i = 3%] Compute FV = $226.39

The bond will be selling at par value of $1,000 in three years, since coupon is forecast to equal yield to maturity. Therefore, total proceeds in three years will be $1,226.39. To find realized compound yield on a semiannual basis (i.e., for six half-year periods), we solve:

$$\$960 \times (1 + y_{realized})^6 = \$1,226.39 \Rightarrow y_{realized} = 4.166\% \text{ (semiannual)}$$

b. Shortcomings of each measure:

(1) Current yield does not account for capital gains or losses on bonds bought at prices other than par value. It also does not account for reinvestment income on coupon payments.

(2) Yield to maturity assumes that the bond is held to maturity and that all coupon income can be reinvested at a rate equal to the yield to maturity.

(3) Realized compound yield (horizon yield) is affected by the forecast of reinvestment rates, holding period, and yield of the bond at the end of the investor's holding period.

30. a. The yield to maturity of the par bond equals its coupon rate, 8.75%. All else equal, the 4% coupon bond would be more attractive because its coupon rate is far below current market yields, and its price is far below the call price. Therefore, if yields fall, capital gains on the bond will not be limited by the call price. In contrast, the 8 3/4% coupon bond can increase in value to at most $1050, offering a maximum possible gain of only 0.5%. The disadvantage of the 8 3/4% coupon bond in terms of vulnerability to a call shows up in its higher *promised* yield to maturity.

b. If an investor expects rates to fall substantially, the 4% bond offers a greater expected return.

c. Implicit call protection is offered in the sense that any likely fall in yields would not be nearly enough to make the firm consider calling the bond. In this sense, the call feature is almost irrelevant.

31. Market conversion price = value if converted into stock = 20.83 × $28 = $583.24

Conversion premium = Bond price – value if converted into stock
= $775 – $583.24 = $191.76

32. a. The call provision requires the firm to offer a higher coupon (or higher promised yield to maturity) on the bond to compensate the investor for the firm's option to call back the bond at a specified call price if interest rates fall sufficiently. Investors are willing to grant this valuable option to the issuer, but only for a price that reflects the possibility that the bond will be called. That price is the higher promised yield at which they are willing to buy the bond.

b. The call option reduces the expected life of the bond. If interest rates fall substantially so that the likelihood of call increases, investors will treat the bond as if it will "mature" and be paid off at the call date, not at the stated maturity date. On the other hand if rates rise, the bond must be paid off at the maturity date, not later. This asymmetry means that the expected life of the bond will be less than the stated maturity.

c. The advantage of a callable bond is the higher coupon (and higher promised yield to maturity) when the bond is issued. If the bond is never called, then an investor will earn a higher realized compound yield on a callable bond issued at par than on a non-callable bond issued at par on the same date. The disadvantage of the callable bond is the risk of call. If rates fall and the bond is called, then the investor receives the call price and will have to reinvest the proceeds at interest rates that are lower than the yield to maturity at which the bond was originally issued. In this event, the firm's savings in interest payments is the investor's loss.

33. a. The forward rate (f_2) is the rate that makes the return from rolling over one-year bonds the same as the return from investing in the two-year maturity bond and holding to maturity:

$$1.08 \times (1 + f_2) = (1.09)^2 \Rightarrow f_2 = 0.1001 = 10.01\%$$

b. According to the expectations hypothesis, the forward rate equals the expected value of the short-term interest rate next year, so the best guess would be 10.01%.

c. According to the liquidity preference hypothesis, the forward rate exceeds the expected short-term interest rate next year, so the best guess would be less than 10.01%.

34. The top row must be the spot rates. The spot rates are (geometric) averages of the forward rates, and the top row is the average of the bottom row. For example, the spot rate on a two-year investment (12%) is the average of the two forward rates 10% and 14.0364%:

$$(1.12)^2 = 1.10 \times 1.140364 = 1.2544$$

35. a. We obtain forward rates from the following table:

Maturity (years)	YTM	Forward rate	Price (for part c)
1	10.0%		$909.09 ($1000/1.10)
2	11.0%	12.01% $[(1.11^2/1.10) - 1]$	$811.62 ($1000/1.11^2$)
3	12.0%	14.03% $[(1.12^3/1.11^2) - 1]$	$711.78 ($1000/1.12^3$)

   b. We obtain next year's prices and yields by discounting each zero's face value at the forward rates derived in part (a):

Maturity (years)	Price		YTM
1	$892.78	[= 1000/1.1201]	12.01%
2	$782.93	[= 1000/(1.1201 x 1.1403)]	13.02%

   Note that this year's upward sloping yield curve implies, according to the expectations hypothesis, a shift upward in next year's curve.

   c. Next year, the two-year zero will be a one-year zero, and it will therefore sell at: ($1000/1.1201) = $892.78
   Similarly, the current three-year zero will be a two-year zero, and it will sell for $782.93.

   Expected total rate of return:

   two-year bond: $\dfrac{\$892.78}{\$811.62} - 1 = 0.1000 = 10.00\%$

   three-year bond: $\dfrac{\$782.93}{\$711.78} - 1 = 0.1000 = 10.00\%$

36. a. A three-year zero with face value $100 will sell today at a yield of 6% and a price of: ($100/1.06^3) =$83.96
   Next year, the bond will have a two-year maturity, and therefore a yield of 6% (reading from next year's forecasted yield curve). The price will be $89.00, resulting in a holding period return of 6%.

   b. The forward rates based on today's yield curve are as follows:

Year		Forward Rate
2	$[(1.05^2/1.04) - 1] =$	6.01%
3	$[(1.06^3/1.05^2) - 1] =$	8.03%

Using the forward rates, the yield curve *next* year is forecast as:

Year	Forward Rate
1	6.01%
2	$[(1.0601 \times 1.0803)^{1/2} - 1] =$ 8.03%

The market forecast is for a higher yield to maturity for two–year bonds than your forecast. Thus, the market predicts a lower price and higher rate of return.

37.   a.   (4) The Euless, Texas, General Obligation Bond, which has been refunded and secured by U.S. Government bonds held in escrow, has as credit quality as good as the U.S. bonds backing it. Euless, Texas has issued new bonds to refund this issue, and, with the proceeds purchased U.S. Government bonds. They did this rather than simply retire the old bonds because the old bonds are not callable yet and because Euless gets to earn the rate on T-bonds while paying a lower rate on its own bonds.

The University of Kansas Medical Center Refunding Revenue Bonds are insured by an entity that is not backed by the taxing power of the U.S. Treasury and therefore the credit quality of these bonds is not as high as the Euless bonds.

The other two bonds have indeterminate quality. Since both are issued by small local governments they may be subject to significant risk. The Sumter, South Carolina, Water and Sewer Revenue Bond is probably less likely to default because the revenues from such essential services are more reliable than the general taxing power of Riley County, Kansas.

   b.   (2) The dividends from the preferred stock are less secure than the interest from the bond.

   c.   (3) The yield on the callable bond must compensate the investor for the risk of call.

Choice (1) is wrong because, although the owner of a callable bond receives principal plus a premium in the event of a call, the interest rate at which he can subsequently reinvest will be low. The low interest rate that makes it profitable for the issuer to call the bond makes it a bad deal for the bond's holder.

Choice (2) is wrong because a bond is more apt to be called when interest rates are low. There will be an interest saving for the issuer only if rates are low.

   d.   (2) is the only correct choice.

(1) is wrong because the yield to maturity is greater than the coupon rate when a bond sells at a discount and is less than the coupon rate when the bond sells at a premium.

(3) is wrong because adding the *average* annual capital gain rate to the current yield does not give the yield to maturity. For example, assume a 10-year bond with a 6% coupon rate, a price of $865.80 and a YTM of 8% per year. The average annual capital gain is: ($1000 − $865.80)/10 years = $13.42
The average annual capital gains rate is: ($13.42/$865.80) = 1.55%

The current coupon yield is: ($60/$865.80) = 0.0693 = 6.93%
Therefore, the "total yield" is: (1.55% + 6.93%) = 8.48%
This is greater than the yield to maturity.

(4) is wrong because yield to maturity is based on the assumption that any payments received are reinvested at the yield to maturity, not at the coupon rate.

e.   (3)

f.   (2)

g.   (4)

CHAPTER 10: MANAGING BOND PORTFOLIOS

1. The percentage bond price change is:

$$-\text{Duration} \times \frac{\Delta y}{1+y} = -7.194 \times \frac{0.0050}{1.10} = -0.0327 \text{ or a 3.27\% decline}$$

2. Computation of duration:

   a. YTM = 6%

(1) Time until Payment (Years)	(2) Payment	(3) Payment Discounted at 6%	(4) Weight	(5) Column (1) x Column (4)
1	60	56.60	0.0566	0.0566
2	60	53.40	0.0534	0.1068
3	1060	890.00	0.8900	2.6700
Column Sum:		1000.00	1.0000	2.8334

   Duration = 2.833 years

   b. YTM = 10%

(1) Time until Payment (Years)	(2) Payment	(3) Payment Discounted at 10%	(4) Weight	(5) Column (1) x Column (4)
1	60	54.55	0.0606	0.0606
2	60	49.59	0.0551	0.1102
3	1060	796.39	0.8844	2.6532
Column Sum:		900.53	1.0000	2.8240

   Duration = 2.824 years, which is less than the duration at the YTM of 6%.

3. Computation of duration, interest rate = 10%:

(1) Time until Payment (Years)	(2) Payment (in millions of dollars)	(3) Payment Discounted at 10%	(4) Weight	(5) Column (1) x Column (4)
1	1	0.9091	0.2744	0.2744
2	2	1.6529	0.4989	0.9978
3	1	0.7513	0.2267	0.6801
	Column Sum:	3.3133	1.0000	1.9523

   Duration = 1.9523 years

4.   The duration of the perpetuity is: $[(1 + y)/y] = (1.10/0.10) = 11$ years. Let w be the weight of the zero-coupon bond. Then we find w by solving:

$$(w \times 1) + [(1 - w) \times 11] = 1.9523 \Rightarrow w = 9.048/10 = 0.9048$$

Therefore, your portfolio should be 90.48% invested in the zero and 9.52% in the perpetuity.

5.   The percentage bond price change will be:

$$- \text{Duration} \times \frac{\Delta y}{1 + y} = -5.0 \times \frac{-0.0010}{1.08} = 0.00463 \text{ or a } .463\% \text{ increase}$$

6.   a.   Bond B has a higher yield to maturity than bond A since its coupon payments and maturity are equal to those of A, while its price is lower. (Perhaps the yield is higher because of differences in credit risk.) Therefore, its duration must be shorter.

     b.   Bond A has a lower yield and a lower coupon, both of which cause it to have a longer duration than that of Bond B. Moreover, Bond A cannot be called. Therefore, the maturity of Bond A is at least as long as that of Bond B, which implies that the duration of Bond A is at least as long as that of Bond B.

7.   C: Highest maturity, zero coupon

     D: Highest maturity, next-lowest coupon

     A: Highest maturity, same coupon as remaining bonds

     B: Lower yield to maturity than bond E

     E: Highest coupon, shortest maturity, highest yield of all bonds.

8.   a. $$\text{Modified duration} = \frac{\text{Macaulay duration}}{1 + \text{YTM}}$$

     If the Macaulay duration is 10 years and the yield to maturity is 8%, then the modified duration is: $(10/1.08) = 9.26$ years

     b.   For option-free coupon bonds, modified duration is better than maturity as a measure of the bond's sensitivity to changes in interest rates. Maturity considers only the final cash flow, while modified duration includes other factors such as the size and timing of coupon payments and the level of interest rates (yield to maturity). Modified duration, unlike maturity, tells us the approximate proportional change in the bond price for a given change in yield to maturity.

     c.   i.   Modified duration increases as the coupon decreases.
          ii. Modified duration decreases as maturity decreases.

9. a. The present value of the obligation is $17,832.65 and the duration is 1.4808 years, as shown in the following table:

Computation of duration, interest rate = 10%:

(1) Time until Payment (Years)	(2) Payment	(3) Payment Discounted at 10%	(4) Weight	(5) Column (1) x Column (4)
1	10,000	9,259.26	0.5192	0.51923
2	10,000	8,573.39	0.4808	0.96154
	Column Sum:	17,832.65	1.0000	1.48077

b. To immunize the obligation, invest in a zero-coupon bond maturing in 1.4808 years. Since the present value of the zero-coupon bond must be $17,832.65, the face value (i.e., the future redemption value) must be:

$$[\$17,832.65 \times (1.08)^{1.4808}] = \$19,985.26$$

c. If the interest rate increases to 9%, the zero-coupon bond would fall in value to:

$$\frac{\$19,985.26}{(1.09)^{1.4808}} = \$17,590.92$$

The present value of the tuition obligation would fall to $17,591.11, so that the net position changes by $0.19.

If the interest rate falls to 7%, the zero-coupon bond would rise in value to:

$$\frac{\$19,985.26}{(1.07)^{1.4808}} = \$18,079.99$$

The present value of the tuition obligation would increase to $18,080.18, so that the net position changes by $0.19.

The reason the net position changes at all is that, as the interest rate changes, so does the duration of the stream of tuition payments.

10. a. PV of obligation = $2 million/0.16 = $12.5 million

Duration of obligation = 1.16/0.16 = 7.25 years

Call w the weight on the five-year maturity bond (with duration of 4 years). Then:

$$(w \times 4) + [(1 - w) \times 11] = 7.25 \Rightarrow w = 0.5357$$

Therefore:

0.5357 × $12.5 = $6.7 million in the 5-year bond, and

0.4643 × $12.5 = $5.8 million in the 20-year bond.

b.   The price of the 20-year bond is:

[60 × Annuity factor(16%,20)] + [1000 × PV factor(16%, 20)] = \$407.12

Therefore, the bond sells for 0.4071 times its par value, so that:

Market value = Par value × 0.4071

\$5.8 million = Par value × 0.4071 $\Rightarrow$ Par value = \$14.25 million

Another way to see this is to note that each bond with par value \$1000 sells for \$407.11. If total market value is \$5.8 million, then you need to buy: (\$5,800,000/407.11) = 14,250 bonds, resulting in total par value of \$14,250,000.

11. a.   The duration of the perpetuity is: (1.05/0.05) = 21 years. Let w be the weight of the zero-coupon bond, so that we find w by solving:

$(w \times 5) + [(1 - w) \times 21] = 10 \Rightarrow w = 11/16 = 0.6875$

Therefore, the portfolio will be 11/16 invested in the zero and 5/16 in the perpetuity.

b.   The zero-coupon bond will then have a duration of 4 years while the perpetuity will still have a 21-year duration. To have a portfolio with duration equal to nine years, which is now the duration of the obligation, we again solve for w:

$(w \times 4) + [(1 - w) \times 21] = 9 \Rightarrow w = 12/17 = 0.7059$

So the proportion invested in the zero increases to 12/17 and the proportion in the perpetuity falls to 5/17.

12. a.   The duration of the perpetuity is: (1.10/0.10) = 11 years. The present value of the payments is: (\$1 million/0.10) = \$10 million. Let w be the weight of the five-year zero-coupon bond and therefore (1 − w) is the weight of the twenty-year zero-coupon bond. Then we find w by solving:

$(w \times 5) + [(1 - w) \times 20] = 11 \Rightarrow w = 9/15 = 0.60$

Therefore, 60% of the portfolio will be invested in the five-year zero-coupon bond and 40% in the twenty-year zero-coupon bond.

Therefore, the market value of the five-year zero is:

\$10 million × 0.60 = \$6 million

Similarly, the market value of the twenty-year zero is:

\$10 million × 0.40 = \$4 million

b.   Face value of the five-year zero-coupon bond is:

$\$6 \text{ million} \times (1.10)^5 = \$9.66 \text{ million}$

Face value of the twenty-year zero-coupon bond is:

$\$4 \text{ million} \times (1.10)^{20} = \$26.91 \text{ million}$

13. While it is true that short-term rates are more volatile than long-term rates, the longer duration of the longer-term bonds makes their rates of return more volatile. The higher duration magnifies the sensitivity to interest-rate savings. Thus, it can be true that *rates* of short-term bonds are more volatile, but the *prices* of long-term bonds are more volatile.

14. a. *Scenario (i)*: Strong economic recovery with rising inflation expectations. Interest rates and bond yields will most likely rise, and the prices of both bonds will fall. The probability that the callable bond will be called declines, so that it will behave more like the non-callable bond. (Notice that they have similar durations when priced to maturity.) The slightly lower duration of the callable bond will result in somewhat better performance in the high interest rate scenario.

   Scenario (ii): Economic recession with reduced inflation expectations. Interest rates and bond yields will most likely fall. The callable bond is likely to be called. The relevant duration calculation for the callable bond is now its modified duration to call. Price appreciation is limited as indicated by the lower duration. The non-callable bond, on the other hand, continues to have the same modified duration and hence has greater price appreciation.

   b. If yield to maturity (YTM) on Bond B falls by 75 basis points:

   Projected price change = (modified duration) × (change in YTM)

   $$= (-6.80) \times (-0.75\%) = 5.1\%$$

   So the price will rise to approximately $105.10 from its current level of $100.

   c. For Bond A (the callable bond), bond life and therefore bond cash flows are uncertain. If one ignores the call feature and analyzes the bond on a "to maturity" basis, all calculations for yield and duration are distorted. Durations are too long and yields are too high. On the other hand, if one treats the premium bond selling above the call price on a "to call" basis, the duration is unrealistically short and yields too low.

   The most effective approach is to use an option valuation approach. The callable bond can be decomposed into two separate securities: a non-callable bond and an option.

   Price of callable bond = Price of non-callable bond – price of option

   Since the option to call the bond always has a positive value, the price of the callable bond is always less than the price of the non-callable security.

15. Using a financial calculator, we find that the price of the bond is:
    For yield to maturity of 7%: $1,620.45
    For yield to maturity of 8%: $1,450.31
    For yield to maturity of 9%: $1,308.21

Using the Duration Rule, assuming yield to maturity falls to 7%:

$$\text{Predicted price change} = -\text{Duration} \times \frac{\Delta y}{1+y} \times P_0$$

$$= -11.54 \times \frac{-0.01}{1.08} \times \$1,450.31 = \$154.97$$

Therefore: Predicted price = $154.97 + $1,450.31 = $1,605.28

The actual price at a 7% yield to maturity is $1,620.45. Therefore:

$$\% \text{ error} = \frac{\$1,620.45 - \$1,605.28}{\$1,620.45} = 0.0094 = 0.94\% \text{ (too low)}$$

Using the Duration Rule, assuming yield to maturity increases to 9%:

$$\text{Predicted price change} = -\text{Duration} \times \frac{\Delta y}{1+y} \times P_0$$

$$= -11.54 \times \frac{+0.01}{1.08} \times \$1,450.31 = -\$154.97$$

Therefore: Predicted price = -$154.97 + $1,450.31 = $1,295.34

The actual price at a 9% yield to maturity is $1,308.21. Therefore:

$$\% \text{ error} = \frac{\$1,308.21 - \$1,295.34}{\$1,308.21} = 0.0098 = 0.98\% \text{ (too low)}$$

Using Duration-with-Convexity Rule, assuming yield to maturity falls to 7%:

$$\text{Predicted price change} = \left[\left(-\text{Duration} \times \frac{\Delta y}{1+y} \right) + \left(0.5 \times \text{Convexity} \times (\Delta y)^2 \right) \right] \times P_0$$

$$= \left[\left(-11.54 \times \frac{-0.01}{1.08} \right) + \left(0.5 \times 192.4 \times (-0.01)^2 \right) \right] \times \$1,450.31 = \$168.92$$

Therefore: Predicted price = $168.92 + $1,450.31 = $1,619.23

The actual price at a 7% yield to maturity is $1,620.45. Therefore:

$$\% \text{ error} = \frac{\$1,620.45 - \$1,619.23}{\$1,620.45} = 0.00075 = 0.075\% \text{ (too low)}$$

Using Duration-with-Convexity Rule, assuming yield to maturity rises to 9%:

$$\text{Predicted price change} = \left[\left(-\text{Duration} \times \frac{\Delta y}{1+y}\right) + \left(0.5 \times \text{Convexity} \times (\Delta y)^2\right)\right] \times P_0$$

$$= \left[\left(-11.54 \times \frac{+0.01}{1.08}\right) + \left(0.5 \times 192.4 \times (0.01)^2\right)\right] \times \$1,450.31 = -\$141.02$$

Therefore: Predicted price = -$141.02 + $1,450.31 = $1,309.29

The actual price at a 9% yield to maturity is $1,308.21. Therefore:

$$\% \text{ error } = \frac{\$1,309.29 - \$1,308.21}{\$1,308.21} = 0.00083 = 0.083\% \text{ (too high)}$$

Conclusion: The duration-with-convexity rule provides more accurate approximations to the actual change in price. In this example, the percentage error using convexity with duration is less than one-tenth the error using duration only to estimate the price change.

16. a. Using a financial calculator, we find that the price of the zero-coupon bond (with $1000 face value) is:
    For yield to maturity of 8%: $374.84
    For yield to maturity of 9%: $333.28

    The price of the 6% coupon bond is:
    For yield to maturity of 8%: $774.84
    For yield to maturity of 9%: $691.79

Zero coupon bond

$$\text{Actual \% loss} = \frac{\$333.28 - \$374.84}{\$374.84} = -0.1109, \text{ an 11.09\% loss}$$

The percentage loss predicted by the duration-with-convexity rule is:

Predicted % loss = $[(-11.81) \times 0.01] + [0.5 \times 150.3 \times (0.01)^2]$

$\qquad\qquad = -0.1106$, an 11.06% loss

Coupon bond

$$\text{Actual \% loss} = \frac{\$691.79 - \$774.84}{\$774.84} = -0.1072, \text{ a 10.72\% loss}$$

The percentage error predicted by the duration-with-convexity rule is:

Predicted % loss = $[(-11.79) \times 0.01] + [0.5 \times 231.2 \times (0.01)^2]$

$\qquad\qquad = -0.1063$, a 10.63% loss

b. Now assume yield to maturity falls to 7%. The price of the zero increases to $422.04, and the price of the coupon bond increases to $875.91.

Zero coupon bond

$$\text{Actual \% gain} = \frac{\$422.04 - \$374.84}{\$374.84} = 0.1259, \text{ a } 12.59\% \text{ gain}$$

The percentage gain predicted by the duration-with-convexity rule is:

Predicted % gain = $[(-11.81) \times (-0.01)] + [0.5 \times 150.3 \times (-0.01)^2]$

$\qquad\qquad\qquad = 0.1256$, a 12.56% gain

Coupon bond

$$\text{Actual \% gain} = \frac{\$875.91 - \$774.84}{\$774.84} = 0.1304, \text{ a } 13.04\% \text{ gain}$$

The percentage gain predicted by the duration-with-convexity rule is:

Predicted % gain = $[(-11.79) \times (-0.01)] + [0.5 \times 231.2 \times (-0.01)^2]$

$\qquad\qquad\qquad = 0.1295$, a 12.95% gain

c. The 6% coupon bond (which has higher convexity) outperforms the zero regardless of whether rates rise or fall. This is a general property which can be understood by first noting from the duration-with-convexity formula that the duration effect resulting from the change in rates is the same for the two bonds because their durations are approximately equal. However, the convexity effect, which is always positive, always favors the higher convexity bond. Thus, if the yields on the bonds always change by equal amounts, as we have assumed in this example, the higher convexity bond always outperforms a lower convexity bond with the same duration and initial yield to maturity.

d. This situation cannot persist. No one would be willing to buy the lower convexity bond if it always underperforms the other bond. The price of the lower convexity bond will fall and its yield to maturity will rise. Thus, the lower convexity bond will sell at a higher initial yield to maturity. That higher yield is compensation for the lower convexity. If rates change only slightly, the higher yield-lower convexity bond will perform better; if rates change by a greater amount, the lower yield-higher convexity bond will do better.

17. a. The Aa bond initially has the higher yield to maturity (yield spread of 40 b.p. versus 31 b.p.), but the Aa bond is expected to have a widening spread relative to Treasuries. This will reduce rate of return. The Aaa spread is expected to be stable. Calculate comparative returns as follows:

Incremental return over Treasuries:
Incremental yield spread − (Change in spread × duration)
Aaa bond: 31 bp − (0 × 3.1) = 31 bp
Aa bond: 40 bp − (10 bp × 3.1) = 9 bp
So choose the Aaa bond.

b. Other variables that one should consider:

• Potential changes in issue-specific credit quality. If the credit quality of the bonds changes, spreads relative to Treasuries will also change.

• Changes in relative yield spreads for a given bond rating. If quality spreads in the general bond market change because of changes in required risk premiums, the yield spreads of the bonds will change even if there is no change in the assessment of the credit quality of these *particular* bonds.

• Maturity effect. As bonds near maturity, the effect of credit quality on spreads can also change. This can affect bonds of different initial credit quality differently.

18. a. 4.

b. 4.

c. 4.

d. 2.

19. a. The two risks are price risk and reinvestment rate risk. The former refers to bond price volatility as interest rates fluctuate, the latter to uncertainty in the rate at which coupon income can be reinvested.

b. Immunization means structuring a bond portfolio so that the value of the portfolio (including proceeds reinvested) will reach a given target level regardless of future changes in interest rates. This is accomplished by matching both the values and durations of the assets and liabilities of the plan. This may be viewed as a low-risk bond management strategy.

c. Duration matching is superior to maturity matching because bonds of equal duration -- not maturity -- are equally sensitive to interest rate fluctuations.

d. Contingent immunization allows for active bond management unless and until the surplus funding in the account is eliminated because of investment losses, at which point an immunization strategy is implemented. Contingent immunization allows for the possibility of above-market returns if the active management is successful.

20. The economic climate is one of impending interest rate increases. Hence, we will want to shorten portfolio duration.

a. Choose the short maturity (2005) bond.

b. The Arizona bond likely has lower duration. Coupons are about equal, but the Arizona yield is higher.

c. Choose the 15 3/8% coupon bond. Maturities are about equal, but the coupon is much higher, resulting in lower duration.

d. The duration of the Shell bond will be lower if the effect of the higher yield to maturity and earlier start of sinking fund redemption dominates the slightly lower coupon rate.

e. The floating rate bond has a duration that approximates the adjustment period, which is only six months.

21. a. This swap would have been made if the investor anticipated a decline in long-term interest rates and an increase in long-term bond prices. The deeper discount, lower coupon 6 3/8% bond would provide more opportunity for capital gains, greater call protection, and greater protection against declining reinvestment rates at a cost of only a modest drop in yield.

b. This swap was probably done by an investor who believed the 24 basis point yield spread between the two bonds was too narrow. The investor anticipated that, if the spread widened to a more normal level, either a capital gain would be experienced on the Treasury note or a capital loss would be avoided on the Phone bond, or both. Also, this swap might have been done by an investor who anticipated a decline in interest rates, and who also wanted to maintain high current coupon income and have the better call protection of the Treasury note. The Treasury note would have unlimited potential for price appreciation, in contrast to the Phone bond which would be restricted by its call price. Furthermore, if intermediate-term interest rates were to rise, the price decline of the higher quality, higher coupon Treasury note would likely be "cushioned" and the reinvestment return from the higher coupons would likely be greater.

c. This swap would have been made if the investor were bearish on the bond market. The zero coupon note would be extremely vulnerable to an increase in interest rates since the yield to maturity, determined by the discount at the time of purchase, is locked in. This is in contrast to the floating rate note, for which interest is adjusted periodically to reflect current returns on debt instruments. The funds received in interest income on the floating rate notes could be used at a later time to purchase long-term bonds at more attractive yields.

d. These two bonds are similar in most respects other than quality and yield. An investor who believed the yield spread between Government and Al bonds was too narrow would have made the swap either to take a capital gain on the Government bond or to avoid a capital loss on the Al bond. The increase in call protection after the swap would not be a factor except under the most bullish interest rate scenarios. The swap does, however, extend maturity another 8 years and yield to maturity sacrifice is 169 basis points.

e. The principal differences between these two bonds are the convertible feature of the Z mart bond and the yield and coupon advantage, and the longer maturity of the Lucky Ducks debentures. The swap would have been made if the investor believed some combination of the following: First, that the appreciation potential of the Z mart convertible, based primarily on the intrinsic value of Z mart common stock, was no longer as attractive as it had been. Second, that the yields on long-term bonds were at a cyclical high, causing bond portfolio managers who could take A2-risk bonds to reach for high yields and long maturities either to lock them in or take a capital gain when rates subsequently declined. Third, while waiting for rates to decline, the investor will enjoy an increase in coupon income. Basically, the investor is swapping an equity-equivalent for a long- term corporate bond.

22. a. A manager who believes that the level of interest rates will change should engage in a rate anticipation swap, lengthening duration if rates are expected to fall, and shortening duration if rates are expected to rise.

   b. A change in yield spreads across sectors would call for an inter-market spread swap, in which the manager buys bonds in the sector for which yields are expected to fall and sells bonds in the sector for which yields are expected to rise.

   c. A belief that the yield spread on a particular instrument will change calls for a substitution swap in which that security is sold if its relative yield is expected to rise or is bought if its yield is expected to fall compared to other similar bonds.

23. Choose the longer-duration bond to benefit from a rate decrease.

   a. The Aaa-rated bond has the lower yield to maturity and therefore the longer duration.

   b. The lower-coupon bond has the longer duration *and* more de facto call protection.

   c. The lower coupon bond has the longer duration.

24. You should buy the three-year bond because it will offer a 9% holding-period return over the next year, which is greater than the return on either of the other bonds, as shown below:

Maturity	One year	Two years	Three years
YTM at beginning of year	7.00%	8.00%	9.00%
Beginning of year price	$1,009.35	$1,000.00	$974.69
End of year price (at 9% YTM)	$1,000.00	$ 990.83	$982.41
Capital gain	-$ 9.35	-$ 9.17	$ 7.72
Coupon	$ 80.00	$ 80.00	$ 80.00
One year total $ return	$ 70.65	$ 70.83	$ 87.72
One year total rate of return	7.00%	7.08%	9.00%

25. The minimum terminal value that the manager is willing to accept is determined by the requirement for a 3% annual return on the initial investment. Therefore, the floor equals: $[\$1 \text{ million} \times (1.03)^5] = \$1.16$ million. Three years after the initial investment, only two years remain until the horizon date, and the interest rate has risen to 8%. Therefore, at this time, in order to be assured that the target value can be attained, the manager needs a portfolio worth:
$[\$1.16 \text{ million}/(1.08)^2] = \$0.995$ million
Therefore, this is the trigger point.

26. The answer depends on the nature of the long-term assets that the corporation is holding. If those assets produce a return that varies with short-term interest rates, then an interest-rate swap would not be appropriate. If, however, the long-term assets are fixed-rate financial assets, such as fixed-rate mortgages, then a swap might reduce risk. In such a case, the corporation would swap its floating-rate bond liability for a fixed-rate long-term liability.

27. The speculator who believes interest rates will fall wants to pay the floating rate and receive the fixed rate. This investor will benefit if the short-term reference rate does in fact fall, resulting in an increase in the net cash flow from the swap.

28. a. In an interest rate swap, one firm exchanges (or "swaps") a fixed payment for another payment that is tied to the level of interest rates. One party in the swap agreement pays a fixed interest rate on the notional principal of the swap. The other party pays the floating interest rate (typically LIBOR) on the same notional principal. For example, in a swap with a fixed rate of 8% and notional principal of $100 million, the *net* cash payment for the firm that pays the fixed rate and receives the floating rate would be: $[(\text{LIBOR} - 0.08) \times \$100 \text{ million}]$. Therefore, if LIBOR exceeds 8%, then this firm receives a payment; if LIBOR is less than 8%, then the firm pays money.

    b. There are several applications of interest rate swaps. For example, suppose that a portfolio manager is holding a portfolio of long-term bonds, but is worried that interest rates might increase, causing a capital loss on the portfolio. This portfolio manager can enter a swap to pay a fixed rate and receive a floating rate, thereby converting the holdings into a synthetic floating rate portfolio. Or, a pension fund manager might identify some money market securities that are paying excellent yields compared to other comparable-risk short-term securities. However, the fund manager might believe that such short-term assets are inappropriate for the portfolio. The fund can hold these securities and enter a swap in which the fund receives a fixed rate and pays a floating rate. The fund thus captures the benefit of the advantageous *relative* yields on these securities, but still establishes a portfolio with interest-rate risk characteristics more like those of long-term bonds.

29. The firm should enter a swap in which it pays a 7% fixed rate and receives LIBOR on $10 million of notional principal. Its total payments will be as follows:

    Interest payments on bond: $(\text{LIBOR} + 0.01) \times \$10$ million par value

    Net cash flow from swap: $(0.07 - \text{LIBOR}) \times \$10$ million notional principal

    TOTAL $\qquad\qquad\qquad 0.08 \times \$10$ million

    The interest rate on the synthetic fixed-rate loan is 8%.

30. The maturity of the 30-year bond will fall to 25 years, and the yield is forecast to be 8%. Therefore, the price forecast for the bond is $893.25 [n = 25; i = 8; FV = 1000; PMT = 70]. At a 6% interest rate, the five coupon payments will accumulate to $394.60 after five years. Therefore, total proceeds will be:
    ($394.60 + $893.25) = $1,287.85
    The five-year return is therefore: $[(\$1,287.85/867.42) - 1] = 1.4847 - 1 = 48.47\%$
    The annual rate of return is: $[(1.4847)^{(1/5)} - 1] = 0.0823 = 8.23\%$

10-12

The maturity of the 20-year bond will fall to 15 years, and its yield is forecast to be 7.5%. Therefore, the price forecast for the bond is $911.73 [n = 15; i = 7.5; FV = 1000; PMT = 65]. At a 6% interest rate, the five coupon payments will accumulate to $366.41 after five years. Therefore, total proceeds will be:
($366.41 + $911.73) = $1,278.14
The five-year return is therefore: [($1,278.14/$879.50) – 1] = 1.4533 – 1 = 45.33%
The annual rate of return is: [(1.4533$^{(1/5)}$ – 1] = 0.0776 = 7.76%
The 30-year bond offers the higher expected return.

31. a. Interest rate = 12%

	Time until Payment (Years)	Payment	Payment Discounted at 12%	Weight	Time x Weight
8% coupon	1	80	71.429	0.0790	0.0790
	2	80	63.776	0.0706	0.1411
	3	1080	768.723	0.8504	2.5513
	Sum:		903.927	1.0000	2.7714
Zero-coupon	1	0	0.000	0.0000	0.0000
	2	0	0.000	0.0000	0.0000
	3	1000	711.780	1.0000	3.0000
	Sum:		711.780	1.0000	3.0000

At a higher discount rate, the weights of the later payments of the coupon bond fall and those of the earlier payments rise. So duration falls. For the zero, the weight of the payment in three years remains at 1.0, and duration therefore remains at 3 years.

b. Continue to use a yield to maturity of 12%

	Time until Payment (Years)	Payment	Payment Discounted at 12%	Weight	Time x Weight
8% coupon	1	120	107.143	0.1071	0.1071
	2	120	95.663	0.0957	0.1913
	3	1120	797.194	0.7972	2.3916
	Sum:		1000.000	1.0000	2.6901

The weights of the earlier payments are higher when the coupon increases. Therefore, duration falls.

32. a.

Time until Payment (Years)	Payment	Payment Discounted at 10%	$t^2 + t$	$t^2 + t$ x PV
1	80	72.727	2	145.455
2	80	66.116	6	396.694
3	1080	811.420	12	9737.040
Sum:		950.263		10279.189

Convexity = [10,279.189/(950.263 × (1.10)^2] = 8.939838

b. At a YTM of 10%, the zero-coupon bond with three-year maturity sells for 751.315 (see Spreadsheet 10.1). Its convexity is:

$$\frac{1}{P \times (1+y)^2} \times \frac{1,000}{(1+y)^t} \times (t^2 + t) = \frac{1}{751.135 \times 1.10^2} \times \frac{1,000}{1.10^3} \times (3^2 + 3) = 9.917355$$

CHAPTER 11: MACROECONOMIC AND INDUSTRY ANALYSIS

1. Expansionary (i.e., looser) monetary policy to lower interest rates would help to stimulate investment and expenditures on consumer durables. Expansionary fiscal policy (i.e., lower taxes, higher government spending, increased welfare transfers) would directly stimulate aggregate demand.

2. a. Gold Mining. Gold is traditionally viewed as a hedge against inflation. Expansionary monetary policy may lead to increased inflation, and could thus enhance the value of gold mining stocks.

    b. Construction. Expansionary monetary policy will lead to lower interest rates, which ought to stimulate housing demand. The construction industry should benefit.

3. A depreciating dollar makes imported cars more expensive and American cars cheaper to foreign consumers. This should benefit the U.S. auto industry.

4. Supply side economists believe that a reduction in income tax rates will make workers more willing to work at current or even slightly lower (gross-of-tax) wages. Such an effect ought to mitigate cost pressures on the inflation rate.

5. a. The robotics process entails higher fixed costs and lower variable (labor) costs. Therefore, this firm will perform better in a boom and worse in a recession. For example, costs will rise less rapidly than revenue when sales volume expands during a boom.

    b. Because its profits are more sensitive to the business cycle, the robotics firm will have the higher beta.

6.

Deep recession	Health care (non-cyclical)
Superheated economy	Steel production (cyclical)
Healthy expansion	Housing construction (cyclical, but interest rate sensitive)
Stagflation	Gold mining (counter cyclical)

7.

a.	Oil well equipment	Decline (environmental pressures, decline in easily-developed oil fields)
b.	Computer hardware	Consolidation stage
c.	Computer software	Consolidation stage
d.	Genetic engineering	Start-up stage
e.	Railroads	Relative decline

8. a. General Autos. Pharmaceutical purchases are less discretionary than automobile purchases.

    b. Friendly Airlines. Travel expenditures are more sensitive to the business cycle than movie consumption.

9. This exercise is left to the student

10. The index of consumer expectations is a useful leading economic indicator because, if consumers are optimistic about the future, then they are more willing to spend money, especially on consumer durables. This spending will increase aggregate demand and stimulate the economy.

11. Labor cost per unit of output is a lagging indicator because wages typically start rising well into an economic expansion. At the beginning of an expansion, there is considerable slack in the economy and output can expand without employers bidding up the price of inputs or the wages of employees. By the time wages start increasing due to high demand for labor, the boom period has already progressed considerably.

12. a. Because of the very short average maturity (30 days), the rate of return on the money market fund will be affected only slightly by changes in interest rates. The fund might be a good place to "park" cash if you forecast an increase in interest rates, especially given the high liquidity of money market funds. The $5,000 can be reinvested in longer-term assets after rates increase.

    b. If you are relatively neutral on rates, the one-year CD might be a reasonable "middle-ground" choice. The CD provides a higher return than the money market fund, unless rates rise considerably. On the other hand, the CD has far less interest rate risk (that is, a much lower duration) than the 20-year bond, and therefore less exposure to interest rate increases.

    c. The long-term bond is the best choice for an investor who wants to speculate on a decrease in rates.

13. a. Relevant data items from the table that support the conclusion that the retail auto parts industry as a whole is in the maturity phase of the industry life cycle are:
    1. The population of 18 to 29-year olds, a major customer base for the industry, is gradually declining.
    2. The number of households with the income less than $35,000, another important consumer base, is not expanding.
    3. The number of cars 5 to 15 years old, an important end market, has experienced low annual growth (and actual declines in some years), so that the number of units potentially in need of parts is not growing.
    4. Automotive aftermarket industry retail sales have been growing slowly for several years.
    5. Consumer expenditures on automotive parts and accessories have grown slowly for several years.
    6. Average operating margins of all retail auto parts companies have steadily declined.

b. Relevant items of data from the table that support the conclusion that Wigwam Autoparts Heaven, Inc. (WAH) and its major competitors are in the consolidation stage of their life cycle are:
1. Sales growth of retail auto parts companies with 100 or more stores have been growing rapidly and at an increasing rate.
2. Market share of retail auto parts stores with 100 or more stores has been increasing, but is still less than 20 percent, leaving room for much more growth.
3. Average operating margins for retail auto parts companies with 100 or more stores are high and rising.

Because of industry fragmentation (i.e., most of the market share is distributed among many companies with only a few stores), the retail auto parts industry apparently is undergoing marketing innovation and consolidation. The industry is moving toward the "category killer" format, in which a few major companies control large market shares through proliferation of outlets. The evidence suggests that a new "industry within an industry" is emerging in the form of the "category killer" large chain-store company. This industry subgroup is in its consolidation stage (i.e., rapid growth with high operating profit margins and emerging market leaders) despite the fact that the industry is in the maturity stage of its life cycle.

14. a. The concept of an industrial life cycle refers to the tendency of most industries to go through various stages of growth. The rate of growth, the competitive environment, profit margins and pricing strategies tend to shift as an industry moves from one stage to the next, although it is usually difficult to pinpoint exactly when one stage has ended and the next begun.

The start-up stage is characterized by perceptions of a large potential market and by high optimism for potential profits. In this stage, however, there is usually a high failure rate. In the second stage, often called rapid growth or consolidation, growth is high and accelerating, markets broaden, unit costs decline and quality improves. In this stage, industry leaders begin to emerge. The third stage, usually called the maturity stage, is characterized by decelerating growth caused by such things as maturing markets and/or competitive inroads by other products. Finally, an industry reaches a stage of relative decline, in which sales slow or even decline.

Product pricing, profitability and industry competitive structure often vary by phase. Thus, for example, the first phase usually encompasses high product prices, high costs (R&D, marketing, etc.) and a (temporary) monopolistic industry structure. In phase two (consolidation stage), new entrants begin to appear and costs fall rapidly due to the learning curve. Prices generally do not fall as rapidly, however, allowing profit margins to increase. In phase three (maturity stage), growth begins to slow as the product or service begins to saturate the market, and margins are eroded by significant price reductions. In the final stage, cumulative industry production is so high that production costs have stopped declining, profit margins are thin (assuming competition exists), and the fate of the industry depends on the extent of replacement demand and the existence of substitute products/services.

b. The passenger car business in the United States has probably entered the final stage in the industrial life cycle because normalized growth is quite low. The information processing business, on the other hand, is undoubtedly earlier in the cycle. Depending on whether or not growth is still accelerating, it is either in the second or third stage.

c. Cars: In the final phases of the life cycle, demand tends to be price sensitive. Thus, Universal can not raise prices without losing volume. Moreover, given the industry's maturity, cost structures are likely to be similar for all competitors, and any price cuts can be matched immediately. Thus, Universal's car business is boxed in: Product pricing is determined by the market, and the company is a "price-taker."

Idata: Idata should have much more pricing flexibility given that it is in an earlier phase of the industrial life cycle. Demand is growing faster than supply, and, depending on the presence and/or actions of an industry leader, Idata may price high in order to maximize current profits and generate cash for product development, or price low in an effort to gain market share.

15. a. A basic premise of the business cycle approach to investing is that stock prices anticipate fluctuations in the business cycle. For example, there is evidence that stock prices tend to move about six months ahead of the economy. In fact, stock prices are a leading indicator for the economy.

Over the course of a business cycle, this approach to investing would work roughly as follows. As the top of a business cycle is perceived to be approaching, stocks purchased should not be vulnerable to a recession. When a downturn is perceived to be at hand, stock holdings should be reduced, with proceeds invested in fixed-income securities. Once the recession has matured to some extent, and interest rates fall, bond prices will rise. As it is perceived that the recession is about to end, profits should be taken in the bonds and proceeds reinvested in stocks, particularly stocks with high beta that are in cyclical industries.

Abnormal returns will generally be earned only if these asset allocation switches are timed better than those of other investors. Switches made after the turning points may not lead to excess returns.

b. Based on the business cycle approach to investment timing, the ideal time to invest in a cyclical stock like a passenger car company would be just before the end of a recession. If the recovery is already underway, Adams's recommendation would be too late. The equities market generally anticipates changes in the economic cycle. Therefore, since the "recovery is underway," the price of Universal Auto should already reflect the anticipated improvements in the economy.

16. a.
- The industry-wide ROE is leveling off, indicating that the industry may be approaching a later stage of the life cycle.
- Average P/E ratios are declining, suggesting that investors are becoming less optimistic about growth prospects.
- Dividend payout is increasing, suggesting that the firm sees less reason to reinvest earnings in the firm. There may be fewer growth opportunities in the industry.
- Industry dividend yield is also increasing, even though market dividend yield is decreasing.

b.
- Industry growth rate is still forecast at 10 – 15%, higher than would be true of a mature industry.
- Non-U.S. markets are still untapped, and some firms are now entering these markets.
- Mail order sale segment is growing at 40% a year.
- Niche markets are continuing to develop.
- New manufacturers continue to enter the market.

17. The expiration of the patent means that General Weedkillers will soon face considerably greater competition from its competitors. We would expect prices and profit margins to fall, and total industry sales to increase somewhat as prices decline. The industry will probably enter the consolidation stage in which producers are forced to compete more extensively on the basis of price.

18. a. (4)
    b. (3)
    c. (3)
    d. (2)
    e. (4)
    f. (3)
    g. (1)

CHAPTER 12: EQUITY VALUATION

1. $P = 2.10/0.11 = 19.09$

2. (a) and (b).

3. a. $P_0 = \dfrac{D_1}{k - g}$

   $$\$50 = \frac{\$2}{0.16 - g} \Rightarrow g = 0.16 - \frac{\$2}{\$50} = 0.12 = 12\%$$

   b. $P_0 = \dfrac{D_1}{k - g} = \dfrac{\$2}{0.16 - 0.05} = \$18.18$

   The price falls in response to the more pessimistic forecast of dividend growth. The forecast for *current* earnings, however, is unchanged. Therefore, the P/E ratio decreases. The lower P/E ratio is evidence of the diminished optimism concerning the firm's growth prospects.

4. a. False. Higher beta means that the risk of the firm is higher and the discount rate applied to value cash flows is higher. For any expected path of earnings and cash flows, the present value of the cash flows, and therefore, the price of the firm will be lower when risk is higher. Thus the ratio of price to earnings will be lower.

   b. True. Higher ROE means more valuable growth opportunities.

   c. Uncertain. The answer depends on a comparison of the expected rate of return on reinvested earnings with the market capitalization rate. If the expected rate of return on the firm's projects is higher than the market capitalization rate, then P/E will increase as the plowback ratio increases.

5. a. $g = ROE \times b = 0.20 \times 0.30 = 0.06 = 6.0\%$

   $D_1 = \$2(1 - b) = \$2(1 - 0.30) = \$1.40$

   $$P_0 = \frac{D_1}{k - g} = \frac{\$1.40}{0.12 - 0.06} = \$23.33$$

   $P/E = \$23.33/\$2 = 11.67$

   b. $PVGO = P_0 - \dfrac{E_0}{k} = \$23.33 - \dfrac{\$2.00}{0.12} = \$6.66$

c. $g = ROE \times b = 0.20 \times 0.20 = = 0.04 = 4.0\%$

$D_1 = \$2(1 - b) = \$2(1 - 0.20) = \$1.60$

$$P_0 = \frac{D_1}{k - g} = \frac{\$1.60}{0.12 - 0.04} = \$20.00$$

$P/E = \$20/\$2 = 10.0$

$$PVGO = P_0 - \frac{E_0}{k} = \$20.00 - \frac{\$2.00}{0.12} = \$3.33$$

6. a. $g = ROE \times b = 0.16 \times 0.5 = 0.08 = 8.0\%$

$D_1 = \$2(1 - b) = \$2(1 - 0.50) = \$1.00$

$$P_0 = \frac{D_1}{k - g} = \frac{\$1.00}{0.12 - 0.08} = \$25.00$$

b. $P_3 = P_0(1 + g)^3 = \$25(1.08)^3 = \$31.49$

7. a. $E(r) = k = \dfrac{D_1}{P_0} + g = \dfrac{0.60}{20} + 0.08 = 0.11 = 11.0\%$

b. The model assumes that the dividend growth rate is constant forever. Therefore, the model cannot be applied to firms that currently do not pay dividends. Second, the model is inappropriate when $g > k$ (which presumably cannot persist indefinitely). Third, the model cannot be applied to firms with variable dividend growth.

c. Two alternative methods are based on P/E multiples and market-to-book multiples exhibited by other firms in the same industry.

8. a. This director is confused. In the context of the constant growth model, it is true that price is higher when dividends are higher *holding everything else (including dividend growth) constant*. But everything else will not be constant. If the firm raises the dividend payout rate, then the growth rate (g) will fall, and stock price will not necessarily rise. In fact, if $ROE > k$, price will fall.

b. An increase in dividend payout reduces the sustainable growth rate as less funds are reinvested in the firm. The sustainable growth rate is (ROE × plowback), which falls as the plowback ratio falls. The increased dividend payout rate reduces the growth rate of book value for the same reason -- less funds are reinvested in the firm.

9. a. $k = r_f + \beta (k_M - r_f) = 6\% + 1.25(14\% - 6\%) = 16\%$

$g = (2/3) \times 9\% = 6\%$

$D_1 = E_0 \times (1 + g) \times (1 - b) = \$3 \times 1.06 \times (1/3) = \$1.06$

$P_0 = \dfrac{D_1}{k - g} = \dfrac{\$1.06}{0.16 - 0.06} = \$10.60$

b. Leading $P_0/E_1 = \$10.60/\$3.18 = 3.33$

Trailing $P_0/E_0 = \$10.60/\$3.00 = 3.53$

c. $PVGO = P_0 - \dfrac{E_0}{k} = \$10.60 - \dfrac{\$3}{.016} = -\$8.15$

The low P/E ratios and negative PVGO are due to a poor ROE (9%) that is less than the market capitalization rate (16%).

d. Now, you revise the following:

$b = 1/3$

$g = 1/3 \times 0.09 = 0.03 = 3.0\%$

$D_1 = E_0 \times 1.03 \times (2/3) = \$2.06$

$V_0 = \dfrac{D_1}{k - g} = \dfrac{\$2.06}{0.16 - 0.06} = \$15.85$

V_0 increases because the firm pays out more earnings instead of reinvesting earnings at a poor ROE. This information is not yet known to the rest of the market.

10. Since $\beta = 1.0$ then k = market return = 15%

Therefore:

$k = \dfrac{D_1}{P_0} + g$

$0.15 = \dfrac{D_1}{P_0} + g = 0.04 + g \Rightarrow g = 0.11 = 11\%$

11. FI Corporation

 a. $P_0 = \dfrac{D_1}{k-g} = \dfrac{\$8.00}{0.10-0.05} = \$160.00$

 b. The dividend payout ratio is $8/12 = 2/3$, so the plowback ratio is $b = (1/3)$. The implied value of ROE on future investments is found by solving as follows:

 $g = b \times ROE$

 $0.05 = (1/3) \times ROE \Rightarrow ROE = 15\%$

 c. Assuming ROE = k, the price is $(E_1/k) \Rightarrow P_0 = \$12/0.10 = \$120$
 Therefore, the market is paying $(\$160 - \$120) = \$40$ per share for growth opportunities.

12. Three different valuation approaches for U.S. Tobacco:

 a. Asset value approach: All of the asset-related per share measures fall below the recent market price, and therefore the stock is not attractive on this basis:

Recent price	$54.00
Book value per share	12.10
Liquidation value per share	9.10
Replacement costs of assets per share	19.50

 b. Constant growth DDM approach: $V_0 = D_1/(k - g) = \$2.10/(0.13 - 0.10) = \$70$

 Thus intrinsic value exceeds market price, so the stock is attractive on this basis.

 c. Earnings multiplier approach: If we apply the P/E multiplier of the S&P 500 to U.S. Tobacco's estimated EPS we get $(23.2 \times \$4.80) = \$111.36$
 This exceeds UST's market price. (Equivalently, UST's P/E ratio is only 11.3, which is considerably less than that of the market.) If you believe that there is no reason for such a large disparity in P/E multiples, you might conclude that the stock is underpriced by the market.

13. High-Flyer stock

 $k = r_f + \beta (k_M - r_f) = 10\% + 1.5(15\% - 10\%) = 17.5\%$

 Therefore:

 $P_0 = \dfrac{D_1}{k-g} = \dfrac{\$2.50}{0.175-0.05} = \$20.00$

14. a. $k = r_f + \beta (k_M - r_f) = 4\% + 1.15 \times (10\% - 4\%) = 10.9\%$

b. Using Emma's short-term growth projections of 25%, we obtain a two-stage DDM value as follows:

$$P_0 = \frac{D_1}{1+k} + \frac{D_2}{(1+k)^2} + \frac{D_3}{(1+k)^3} + \frac{D_4 + D_5/(k-g)}{(1+k)^4}$$

$$= \frac{0.287}{1.109} + \frac{0.359}{1.109^2} + \frac{0.449}{1.109^3} + \frac{0.561 + [0.701/(0.109 - 0.093)]}{1.109^4}$$

$$= 0.259 + 0.292 + 0.329 + 29.336 = \$30.216$$

c. With these new assumptions, Disney stock has an intrinsic value less than the market price of $37.75. This analysis indicates a sell recommendation. Even though Disney's five-year growth rate increases, beta and the risk premium also increase. The intrinsic value falls.

15. a. It is true that NewSoft sells at higher multiples of earnings and book value than Capital. But this difference may be justified by NewSoft's higher expected growth rate of earnings and dividends. NewSoft is in a growing market with abundant profit and growth opportunities. Capital is in a mature industry with fewer growth prospects. Both the price-earnings and price-book ratios reflect the prospect of growth opportunities, indicating that the ratios for these firms do not necessarily imply mispricing.

b. The most important weakness of the constant-growth dividend discount model in this application is that it assumes a perpetual constant growth rate of dividends. While dividends may be on a steady growth path for Capital, which is a more mature firm, that is far less likely to be a realistic assumption for NewSoft.

c. NewSoft should be valued using a multi-stage DDM, which allows for rapid growth in the early years, but also recognizes that growth must ultimately slow to a more sustainable rate.

16.

		Stock A	Stock B
a.	Dividend payout ratio = 1 − b	$1/$2 = 0.50	$1/$1.65 = 0.606
b.	Growth rate = g = ROE × b	0.14 × 0.5 = 7.0%	0.12 × 0.394 = 4.728%
c.	Intrinsic value = V_0	$1/(0.10 − 0.07)	$1/(0.10 − 0.04728)
		= $33.33	= $18.97

d. You would choose to invest in Stock A since its intrinsic value exceeds its price. You might choose to sell short stock B.

17. a. $k = r_f + \beta\,[E(r_M) - r_f] = 4.5\% + 1.15(14.5\% - 4.5\%) = 16\%$

b.

Year	Dividends	
1999	$1.72	
2000	1.72×1.12	= $1.93
2001	1.72×1.12^2	= $2.16
2002	1.72×1.12^3	= $2.42
2003	$1.72 \times 1.12^3 \times 1.09$	= $2.64

Present value of dividends paid in years 2000 to 2002:

Year	PV of Dividends
2000	$1.93/1.16^1 = 1.66
2001	$2.16/1.16^2 = 1.61
2002	$2.42/1.16^3 = 1.55
	Total: $4.82

Price at year-end 2002 $= P_{2002} = \dfrac{D2003}{k-g} = \dfrac{\$2.64}{0.16 - 0.09} = \$37.71$

PV (in 1999) of $P_{2002} = \$37.71/(1.16^3) = \$24.16$

Intrinsic value of stock = $4.82 + $24.16 = $28.98

c. The table presented in the problem indicates that Quick Brush is selling below intrinsic value, while we have just shown that Smile White is selling somewhat above the estimated intrinsic value. Based on this analysis, Quick Brush offers the potential for considerable abnormal returns, while Smile White offers slightly below-market risk-adjusted returns.

d. Strengths of two-stage DDM compared to constant growth DDM:

- The two-stage model allows for separate valuation of two distinct periods in a company's future. This approach can accommodate life cycle effects. It also can avoid the difficulties posed when the initial growth rate is higher than the discount rate.

- The two-stage model allows for an initial period of above-sustainable growth. It allows the analyst to make use of her expectations as to when growth may shift to a more sustainable level.

  A weakness of all DDMs is that they are all very sensitive to input values. Small changes in k or g can imply large changes in estimated intrinsic value. These inputs are difficult to measure.

18. Tennant Company

$D_0 = \$0.96$ $E_0 = \$1.85$ $ROE = \$1.85/\$13.07 = 0.142$

Dividend payout = $\$0.96/\$1.85 = 0.519$

Plowback ratio = $b = 0.481$

$g = b \times ROE = 0.481 \times 0.142 = 0.068 = 6.8\%$

$k = 7\% + 5\% = 12\%$

a. $V_0 = \dfrac{D_1}{k - g} = \dfrac{\$0.96 \times 1.068}{0.12 - 0.068} = \$19.72$

b.   If ROE = 20% and b = 0.65 then g = (0.20 × 0.65) = 13%, which is greater than k. Whenever g > k, the constant growth rate DDM produces a meaningless result since it gives a negative value for the value of the stock. You would therefore need to try a multistage DDM.

19. Nucor Corporation

a.   The expected return on the stock market is the bond yield plus the risk premium of stocks over bonds: $E(r_M) = 9\% + 5\% = 14\%$

b.   First we calculate ROE in order to find g. ROE is the estimated EPS divided by estimated book value:

   ROE = $\$4.25/\$25 = 0.17 = 17\%$

   Dividend payout ratio = $\$0.40/\$4.25 = 0.094$

   $b = 1 - 0.094 = 0.906$

   $g = b \times ROE = 0.906 \times 17\% = 15.4\%$

   Implied total return = Dividend yield + g = ($\$0.40/\$53$) + 0.154

                     = 0.162 = 16.2%

c.   Required return = $r_f + \beta\ [E(r_M) - r_f] = 7\% + 1.1(14\% - 7\%) = 14.7\%$

d.   Nucor's implied total return exceeds the required return derived from the CAPM. This suggests that Nucor stock is undervalued, so that it is an attractive investment.

20. <u>Nogro Corporation</u>

   a. $D_1 = 0.5 \times \$2 = \$1$

   $g = b \times ROE = 0.5 \times 0.20 = 0.10$

   Therefore:

   $$k = \frac{D_1}{P_0} + g = \frac{\$1}{\$10} + 0.10 = 0.20 = 20.0\%$$

   b. Since k = ROE, the NPV of future investment opportunities is zero:

   $$PVGO = P_0 - \frac{E_0}{k} = \$10 - \$10 = \$0$$

   c. Since k = ROE, the stock price would be unaffected if Nogro were to cut its dividend payout ratio to 25%. The additional earnings that would be reinvested would earn the ROE (20%).

   Again, if Nogro eliminated the dividend, this would have no impact on Nogro's stock price since the NPV of the additional investments would be zero.

21. <u>Xyrong Corporation</u>

   a. $k = r_f + \beta[E(r_M) - r_f] = 8\% + 1.2(15\% - 8\%) = 16.4\%$

   $g = b \times ROE = 0.6 \times 0.20 = 12\%$

   $$V_0 = \frac{D_0 \times (1 + g)}{k - g} = \frac{\$4 \times 1.12}{0.164 - 0.12} = \$101.82$$

   b. $P_1 = V_1 = V_0 \times (1 + g) = 101.82 \times 1.12 = \$114.04$

   $$E(r) = \frac{D_1 + P_1 - P_0}{P_0} = \frac{\$4.48 + \$114.04 - \$100}{\$100} = 0.1852 = 18.52\%$$

CHAPTER 13: FINANCIAL STATEMENT ANALYSIS

1. ROA = ROS × ATO

    The only way that Crusty Pie can have an ROS higher than the industry average and an ROA equal to the industry average is for its ATO to be lower than the industry average.

2. ABC's asset turnover must be above the industry average.

3. From Equation 13.1:

    $$ROE = (1 - \text{Tax rate})\left[ROA + (ROA - \text{Interest rate})\frac{\text{Debt}}{\text{Equity}} \right]$$

    We know that $ROE_A > ROE_B$ and that Firms A and B have the same ROA. Assuming the two firms have the same tax rate, then they must have different interest rates and/or debt ratios.

4. (c) Old plant and equipment is likely to have a low net book value, making the ratio of "net sales to average net fixed assets" higher.

5. This transaction would increase the current ratio will. The transaction reduces both current assets and current liabilities by the same amount, but the reduction has a larger proportionate impact on current liabilities than on current assets. Therefore, the current ratio would increase.

    This transaction would increase the asset turnover ratio. Sales should remain unaffected, but assets are reduced.

6. SmileWhite has the higher quality of earnings for several reasons:

    - SmileWhite amortizes its goodwill over a shorter period than does QuickBrush. SmileWhite therefore presents more conservative earnings because it has greater goodwill amortization expense.
    - SmileWhite depreciates its property, plant and equipment using an accelerated method. This results in earlier recognition of depreciation expense, so that income is more conservatively stated.
    - SmileWhite's bad debt allowance, as a percent of receivables, is greater. SmileWhite therefore recognizes higher bad-debt expense than does QuickBrush. If the actual collection experience for the two firms is comparable, then SmileWhite has the more conservative recognition policy.

7. $$ROE = \frac{\text{Net profit}}{\text{equity}} = 5.5\% \times 2.0 \times 2.2 = 24.2\%$$

8.

Par value	20,000 x $20 =	$ 400,000
Retained earnings		5,000,000
Addition to Retained earnings		70,000
Book value of equity		$5,470,000

Book value per share = $5,470,000/20,000 = $273.50

9. a.

Palomba Pizza Stores
Statement of Cash Flows
For Year Ended December 31, 2001

Cash flows from operating activities		
Cash collections from customers	$250,000	
Cash payments to suppliers	(85,000)	
Cash payments for Salaries	(45,000)	
Cash payments for interest	(10,000)	
Net cash provided by operating activities		$110,000
Cash flows from investing activities		
Sale of equipment	38,000	
Purchase of equipment	(30,000)	
Purchase of land	(14,000)	
Net cash provided by (used in) investing activities		$ (6,000)
Cash flows from financing activities		
Retirement of commons stock	(25,000)	
Payment of dividends	(35,000)	
Net cash provided by (used in) financing activities		$(60,000)
Net increase in cash		44,000
Cash at beginning of year		50,000
Cash at end of year		$ 94,000

b. Cash flow from operations (CFO) focuses on measuring the cash flow generated by operations, not on measuring profitability. If used as a measure of performance, CFO is less subject to distortion than the net income figure. Analysts use the CFO as a check on the quality of earnings. The CFO then becomes a check on the reported net earnings figure, although not as a substitute for net earnings. Companies with high net income but low CFO may be using income recognition techniques that are suspect. The ability of a firm to generate cash from operations on a consistent basis is one indication of the financial health of the firm. For most firms, CFO is the "life blood" of the firm. Analysts search for trends in CFO to indicate future cash conditions and the potential for cash flow problems.

Cash flow from investing activities (CFI) is an indication of how the firm is investing its excess cash. The analyst must consider the ability of the firm to continue to grow and expand activities; CFI is a good indication of the attitude of management in this area. Analysis of this component of total cash flow indicates the type of capital expenditures being made by management to either expand or maintain productive capability. CFI is also an indicator of the firm's financial flexibility and its ability to generate sufficient cash to respond to unanticipated needs and opportunities. Decreasing CFI may be a sign of a slowdown in growth of the firm.

Cash flow from financing activities (CFF) presents the feasibility of financing, the sources of financing, and an indication of the types of sources management supports. Continued debt financing may signal a future cash flow problem. The dependency of a firm on external sources of financing (either debt or equity financing) may present troubles in the future with regard to debt servicing and maintaining dividend policy. Analysts also use CFF as an indication of the quality of earnings. It offers insights into the financial habits of management and potential future policies.

10. <u>Chicago Refrigerator Co.</u>

a. $$\text{Quick Ratio} = \frac{\text{Cash} + \text{receivables}}{\text{Current liabilities}} = \frac{\$325 + \$3599}{\$3945} = 0.99$$

b. $$\text{ROA} = \frac{\text{EBIT}}{\text{Assets}} = \frac{\text{Net income before tax} + \text{interest expense}}{\text{Average assets}}$$

$$= \frac{\$2259 + \$78}{0.5 \times (\$8058 + \$4792)} = 0.364 = 36.4\%$$

c. $$\text{ROE} = \frac{\text{Net income} - \text{preferred dividends}}{\text{Average common equity}}$$

Preferred dividends $= 0.1 \times \$25 \times 18{,}000 = \$45{,}000$

Common equity in 1999 $= \$829 + \$575 + \$1{,}949 = \$3{,}353$ million

Common equity in 1998 $= \$550 + \$450 + \$1{,}368 = \$2{,}368$ million

$$\text{ROE} = \frac{\text{Net income} - \text{preferred dividends}}{\text{Average common equity}} = \frac{\$1265 - \$45}{0.5 \times (\$3353 + \$2368)} = 0.426 = 42.6\%$$

d. $$\text{Earnings per share} = \frac{\$1265 - \$45}{0.5 \times (829 + 550)} = \$1.77$$

e. $$\text{Profit margin} = \frac{\text{EBIT}}{\text{Sales}} = \frac{\$2259 + \$78}{\$12065} = 0.194 = 19.4\%$$

f. $$\text{Times interest earned} = \frac{\text{EBIT}}{\text{Interest expense}} = \frac{\$2259 + \$78}{\$78} = 30.0$$

g. $$\text{Inventory turnover} = \frac{\text{Cost of goods sold}}{\text{Average inventory}} = \frac{\$8048}{0.5 \times (\$1415 + \$2423)} = 4.19$$

h. $$\text{Leverage ratio} = \frac{\text{Average assets}}{\text{Average common equity}} = \frac{0.5 \times (\$4792 + \$8058)}{0.5 \times (\$2368 + \$3353)} = 2.25$$

11. a.

12. a.

13. b.

14. a. [The use of FIFO during a period of deflation means that higher-historical-cost goods are "taken out of inventory." So accounting income is lower and assets are lower.]

15. a.

$$\text{ROE} = \frac{\text{Net profit}}{\text{Equity}} = \frac{\text{Net profit}}{\text{Pretax profit}} \times \frac{\text{Pretax profit}}{\text{EBIT}} \times \frac{\text{EBIT}}{\text{Sales}} \times \frac{\text{Sales}}{\text{Assets}} \times \frac{\text{Assets}}{\text{Equity}}$$

= Tax-burden × Interest burden × Profit margin × Asset turnover × Leverage

$$\text{Tax burden} = \frac{\text{Net profit}}{\text{Pretax Profit}} = \frac{\$510}{\$805} = 0.6335$$

$$\text{Interest burden} = \frac{\text{Pretax profit}}{\text{EBIT}} = \frac{\$805}{\$830} = 0.9699$$

$$\text{Profit margin} = \frac{\text{EBIT}}{\text{Sales}} = \frac{\$830}{\$5140} = 0.1615$$

$$\text{Asset turnover} = \frac{\text{Sales}}{\text{Assets}} = \frac{\$5140}{\$3100} = 1.6581$$

$$\text{Leverage} = \frac{\text{Assets}}{\text{Equity}} = \frac{\$3100}{\$2200} = 1.4091$$

b. ROE = 0.6335 × 0.9699 × 0.1615 × 1.6581 × 1.4091 = 0.2318 = 23.18%

c. $g = \text{ROE} \times \text{plowback} = 0.2318 \times \frac{1.96 - 0.60}{1.96} = 0.1608 = 16.08\%$

16. c

17. c

18. a. QuickBrush has had higher sales and earnings growth (per share) than SmileWhite. Margins are also higher. But this does not necessarily mean that QuickBrush is a better investment. SmileWhite has a higher ROE, which has been stable, while QuickBrush's ROE has been declining. We can use Du Pont analysis to identify the source of the difference in ROE:

Component	Definition	QuickBrush	SmileWhite
Tax burden (1 − t)	Net profit/Pretax profit	67.4%	66.0%
Interest burden	Pretax profit/EBIT	1.00	0.955
Profit margin	EBIT/Sales	8.5%	6.5%
Asset turnover	Sales/Assets	1.42	3.55
Leverage	Assets/Equity	1.47	1.48
ROE	Net profit/Equity	12.0%	21.4%

While tax burden, interest burden, and leverage are similar, profit margin and asset turnover differ. Although SmileWhite has a lower profit margin, it has far higher asset turnover.

Sustainable growth = ROE × plowback ratio

	ROE	Plowback ratio	Sustainable growth rate	Ludlow's estimate
QuickBrush	12.0%	1.00	12.0%	30.0%
SmileWhite	21.4%	0.34	7.3%	10.0%

Ludlow has overestimated the sustainable growth rate for each company. QuickBrush has little ability to increase its sustainable growth because plowback already equals 100%. SmileWhite could increase its sustainable growth by increasing its plowback ratio.

  b. QuickBrush's recent EPS growth has been achieved by increasing book value per share, not by achieving greater profits per dollar of equity. Since EPS is equal to (Book value per share × ROE), a firm can increase EPS even if ROE is declining; this is the case for QuickBrush. QuickBrush's book value per share has more than doubled in the last two years.

Book value per share can increase either by retaining earnings or by issuing new stock at a market price greater than book value. QuickBrush has been retaining all earnings, but the increase in the number of outstanding shares indicates that it has also issued a substantial amount of stock.

19.

		1998	2002

Operating margin $= \dfrac{\text{Operating income - depreciation}}{\text{Sales}}$ $\qquad \dfrac{38-3}{542} = 6.5\%$ $\qquad \dfrac{76-9}{979} = 6.8\%$

Asset turnover $= \dfrac{\text{Sales}}{\text{Total Assets}}$ $\qquad \dfrac{542}{245} = 2.21$ $\qquad \dfrac{979}{291} = 3.36$

Interest Burden $= \dfrac{\text{Pretax income}}{\text{Operating income} - \text{Depreciation}}$ $\qquad \dfrac{32}{38-3} = 0.914$ $\qquad \dfrac{67}{76-9} = 1.00$

Financial Leverage $= \dfrac{\text{Total Assets}}{\text{Shareholders' Equity}}$ $\qquad \dfrac{245}{159} = 1.54$ $\qquad \dfrac{291}{220} = 1.32$

Income tax rate $= \dfrac{\text{Income taxes}}{\text{Pretax income}}$ $\qquad \dfrac{13}{32} = 40.63\%$ $\qquad \dfrac{37}{67} = 55.22\%$

Using the Du Pont formula:

ROE(1998) = (1 – 0.4063) × 0.914 × 0.065 × 2.21 × 1.54 = 0.120 = 12.0%

ROE(2002) = (1 - 0.5522) × 1.0 × 0.068 × 3.36 × 1.32 = 0.135 = 13.5%

b. (i) Asset turnover measures the ability of a company to minimize the level of assets (current or fixed) to support its level of sales. The asset turnover increased substantially over the period, thus contributing to an increase in the ROE.

(ii) Financial leverage measures the amount of financing, not including equity, but including short and long-term debt, that the firm uses. Financial leverage declined over the period thus adversely affected the ROE. Since asset turnover increased substantially more than financial leverage declined, the net effect was an increase in ROE.

CHAPTER 14: OPTIONS MARKETS

1. c is false. This is the description of the payoff to a put, not a call.

2. c is the only correct statement.

3. Each contract is for 100 shares: $7.25 \times 100 = \$725$

4.

	Cost	Payoff	Profit
Call option, X = 65	4.50	5.00	+0.50
Put option, X = 65	0.70	0.00	-0.70
Call option, X = 70	1.35	0.00	-1.35
Put option, X = 70	2.45	0.00	-2.45
Call option, X = 75	0.30	0.00	-0.30
Put option, X = 75	6.30	5.00	-1.30

5. In terms of dollar returns:

	Price of Stock Six Months From Now			
Stock price:	80	100	110	120
All stocks (100 shares)	8,000	10,000	11,000	12,000
All options (1,000) shares	0	0	10,000	20,000
Bills + 100 options	9,360	9,360	10,360	11,360

In terms of rate of return, based on a $10,000 investment:

	Price of Stock Six Months From Now			
Stock price:	80	100	110	120
All stocks (100 shares)	-20%	0%	10%	20%
All options (1,000) shares	-100%	-100%	0%	100%
Bills + 100 options	-6.4%	-6.4%	3.6%	13.6%

14-1

6. a. Purchase a straddle, i.e., both a put and a call on the stock. The total cost of the straddle would be: ($10 + $7) = $17

    b. Since the straddle costs $17, this is the amount by which the stock would have to move in either direction for the profit on either the call or put to cover the investment cost (not including time value of money considerations).

7. a. Sell a straddle, i.e., sell a call *and* a put to realize premium income of: ($4 + $7) = $11

    b. If the stock ends up at $50, both of the options will be worthless and your profit will be $11. This is your maximum possible profit since, at any other stock price, you will have to pay off on either the call or the put. The stock price can move by $11 (your initial revenue from writing the two at-the-money options) in either direction before your profits become negative.

    c. Buy the call, sell (write) the put, lend the present value of $50. The payoff is as follows:

		Final Payoff	
Position	Initial Outlay	$S_T < X$	$S_T > X$
Long call	$C = 7$	0	$S_T - 50$
Short put	$-P = -4$	$-(50 - S_T)$	0
Lending	$50/(1 + r)^{(1/4)}$	50	50
Total	$7 - 4 + [50/(1 + r)^{(1/4)}]$	S_T	S_T

    The initial outlay equals: [(the present value of $50) + $3]. In either scenario, you end up with the same payoff as you would if you bought the stock itself.

8. a. By writing covered call options, Jones receives premium income of $30,000. If, in January, the price of the stock is less than or equal to $45, he will keep the stock plus the premium income. But the *most* he can have is $450,000 + $30,000 because the stock will be called away from him if its price exceeds $45. (We are ignoring interest earned on the premium income from writing the option over this short time period.) The payoff structure is:

Stock price	Portfolio value
Less than $45	(10,000 times stock price) + $30,000
Greater than $45	$450,000 + $30,000 = $480,000

    This strategy offers some premium income but leaves the investor with substantial downside risk. At the extreme, if the stock price falls to zero, Jones would be left with only $30,000. This strategy also puts a cap on the final value at $480,000, but this is more than sufficient to purchase the house.

    b. By buying put options with a $35 strike price, Jones will be paying $30,000 in premiums in order to insure a minimum level for the final value of his position. That minimum value is: [($35 × 10,000) − $30,000] = $320,000. This strategy allows for upside gain, but exposes Jones to the possibility of a moderate loss equal to the cost of the puts. The payoff structure is:

Stock price	Portfolio value
Less than $35	$350,000 − $30,000 = $320,000
Greater than $35	(10,000 times stock price) − $30,000

14-2

c. The net cost of the collar is zero. The value of the portfolio will be as follows:

Stock price	Portfolio value
Less than $35	$350,000
Between $35 and $45	10,000 times stock price
Greater than $45	$450,000

If the stock price is less than or equal to $35, then the collar preserves the $350,000 in principal. If the price exceeds $45, then Jones gains up to a cap of $450,000. In between $35 and $45, his proceeds equal 10,000 times the stock price.

The best strategy in this case is (c) since it satisfies the two requirements of preserving the $350,000 in principal while offering a chance of getting $450,000. Strategy (a) should be ruled out because it leaves Jones exposed to the risk of substantial loss of principal.

Our ranking is: (1) c   (2) b (3) a

9.   a.   Butterfly Spread

Position	$S < X_1$	$X_1 < S < X_2$	$X_2 < S < X_3$	$X_3 < S$
Long call (X_1)	0	$S - X_1$	$S - X_1$	$S - X_1$
Short 2 calls (X_2)	0	0	$-2(S - X_2)$	$-2(S - X_2)$
Long call (X_3)	0	0	0	$S - X_3$
Total	0	$S - X_1$	$2X_2 - X_1 - S$	$(X_2-X_1) - (X_3-X_2) = 0$

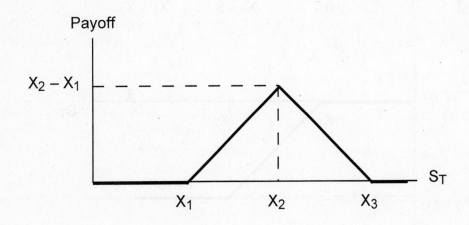

b.   Vertical combination

Position	$S < X_1$	$X_1 < S < X_2$	$S > X_2$
Long call (X_2)	0	0	$S - X_2$
Long put (X_1)	$X_1 - S$	0	0
Total	$X_1 - S$	0	$S - X_2$

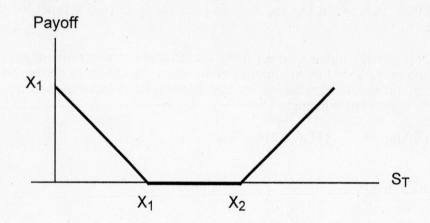

10.   Bear spread

Position	$S < X_1$	$X_1 < S < X_2$	$S > X_2$
Long call (X_2)	0	0	$S - X_2$
Short call (X_1)	0	$-(S - X_1)$	$-(S - X_1)$
Total	0	$X_1 - S$	$X_1 - X_2$

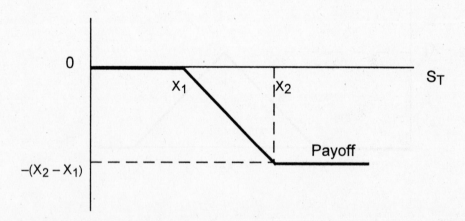

In the bullish spread, the payoff either increases or is unaffected by stock price increases. In the bearish spread, the payoff either increases or is unaffected by stock price *decreases*.

11. a.

Protective Put	$S_T < 1040$	$S_T > 1040$
Stock	S_T	S_T
Put	$1040 - S_T$	0
Total	1040	S_T

Bills and Call	$S_T < 1120$	$S_T > 1120$
Bills	1120	1120
Call	0	$S_T - 1120$
Total	1120	S_T

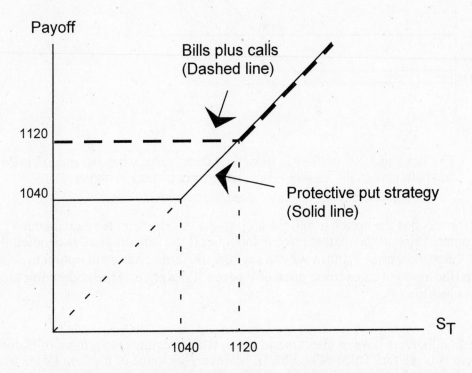

b. The bills plus call strategy has a greater payoff for some values of S_T and never a lower payoff. Since its payoffs are always at least as attractive and sometimes greater, it must be more costly to purchase.

c. The initial cost of the stock plus put position is 1,208 and the cost of the bills plus call position is 1,240.

Position	$S_T = 0$	$S_T = 1040$	$S_T = 1120$	$S_T = 1200$	$S_T = 1280$
Stock	0	1040	1120	1200	1280
+ Put	1040	0	0	0	0
Payoff	1040	1040	1120	1200	1280
Profit	-168	-168	-88	-8	+72

Position	$S_T = 0$	$S_T = 1040$	$S_T = 1120$	$S_T = 1200$	$S_T = 1280$
Bill	1120	1120	1120	1120	1120
+ Call	0	0	0	80	160
Payoff	1120	1120	1120	1200	1280
Profit	-120	-120	-120	-40	+40

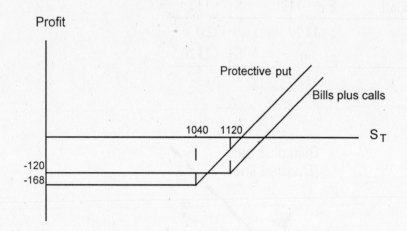

d.   The stock and put strategy is riskier. It does worse when the market is down, and better when the market is up. Therefore, its beta is higher.

12.   The farmer has the option to sell the crop to the government, for a guaranteed minimum price, if the market price is too low. If the support price is denoted P_S and the market price P_m then we can say that the farmer has a put option to sell the crop (the asset) at an exercise price of P_S even if the price of the underlying asset (P) is less than P_S.

13.   The bondholders have in effect made a loan which requires repayment of B dollars, where B is the face value of bonds. If, however, the value of the firm (V) is less than B, then the loan is satisfied by the bondholders taking over the firm. In this way, the bondholders are forced to "pay" B (in the sense that the loan is cancelled) in return for an asset worth only V. It is as though the bondholders wrote a put on an asset worth V, with exercise price B. Alternatively, one can view the bondholders as giving to the equityholders the right to reclaim the firm by paying off the B dollar debt. The bondholders have issued a call to the equity holders.

14.   The executive receives a bonus if the stock price exceeds a certain value, and receives nothing otherwise. This is the same as the payoff to a call option.

15. a.

Position	$S < 70$	$70 < S < 75$	$S > 75$
Short call	0	0	$-(S - 75)$
Short put	$-(70 - S)$	0	0
Total	$S - 70$	0	$75 - S$

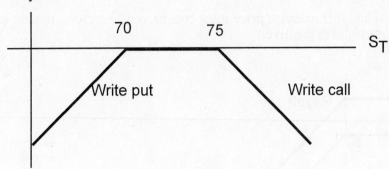

b. Proceeds from writing options (from Figure 14.1):

Call = $0.30

Put = $2.45

Total = $2.75

If Microsoft is selling at $72, both options expire out of the money, and profit equals $2.75. If Microsoft is selling at $80, the call written results in a cash outflow of $5 at maturity, and an overall profit of: ($2.75 – $5.00) = –$2.25

c. You break even when *either* the put *or* the call written results in a cash outflow of $2.75. For the put, this requires that:

$2.75 = $70 – S \Rightarrow S = $72.75

For the call this requires that:

$2.75 = S – $75 \Rightarrow S = $77.75

d. The investor is betting that Microsoft stock price will have low volatility. This position is similar to a straddle.

16. a. If an investor buys a call option and writes a put option on a T-bond, then, at maturity, the total payoff to the position is $(S_T - X)$, where S_T is the price of the T-bond at the maturity date (time T). This is equivalent to the profit on a forward or futures position with futures price X. If you choose an exercise price (X) equal to the current T-bond futures price, then the profit on the portfolio replicates that of market-traded futures.

b. Such a position would increase the portfolio duration, just as adding a T-bond futures contract increases duration. As interest rates fall, the portfolio increases in value, so that duration is longer than it was before the synthetic futures position was established.

c. Futures can be bought and sold very cheaply and quickly. They give the manager flexibility to pursue strategies or particular bonds that seem attractively priced without worrying about the impact of these actions on portfolio duration. The futures can be used to make adjustments to duration necessitated by other portfolio actions.

17. The put with the higher exercise price must cost more. Therefore, the net outlay to establish the portfolio is positive.

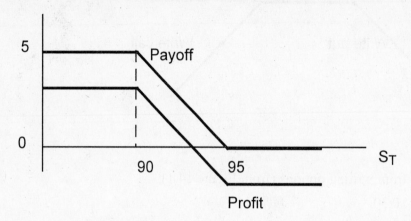

18. Buy the X = 62 put (which should cost more than it does) and write the X = 60 put. Since the options have the same price, the net outlay is zero. Your proceeds at maturity may be positive, but cannot be negative.

Position	$S_T < 60$	$60 < S_T < 62$	$S_T > 62$
Long put (X = 62)	$62 - S_T$	$62 - S_T$	0
Short put (X = 60)	$-(60 - S_T)$	0	0
Total	2	$62 - S_T$	0

Payoff = Profit (because net investment = 0)

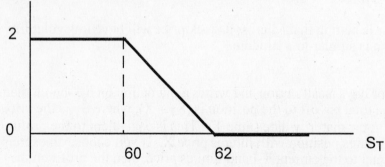

19. The following payoff table shows that the portfolio is riskless with time-T value equal to \$10. Therefore, the risk-free rate is: $[(\$10/\$9.50) - 1] = 0.0526 = 5.26\%$

Position	$S_T < 10$	$S_T > 10$
Buy stock	S_T	S_T
Short call	0	$-(S_T - 10)$
Long put	$10 - S_T$	0
Total	10	10

20. a. <u>Joe's strategy</u>

		Final Payoff	
Position	Initial Outlay	$S_T < 1200$	$S_T > 1200$
Stock index	1200	S_T	S_T
Long put (X = 1200)	60	$1200 - S_T$	0
Total	1260	1200	S_T
Profit = payoff - 1260		-60	$S_T - 1260$

<u>Sally's Strategy</u>

		Final Payoff	
Position	Initial Outlay	$S_T < 1170$	$S_T > 1170$
Stock index	1200	S_T	S_T
Long put (X = 1170)	45	$1170 - S_T$	0
Total	1260	1170	S_T
Profit = payoff - 1245		-75	$S_T - 1245$

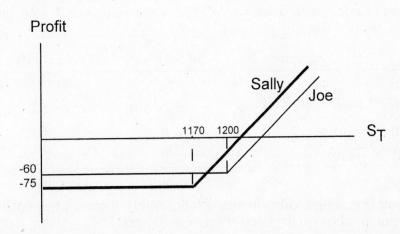

b. Sally does better when the stock price is high, but worse when the stock price is low. (The break-even point occurs at S = \$1185, when both positions provide losses of \$60.)

c. Sally's strategy has greater systematic risk. Profits are more sensitive to the value of the stock index.

21. This strategy is a bear spread. The initial proceeds are: ($9 – $3) = $6. The payoff is either negative or zero:

Position	$S_T < 50$	$50 < S_T < 60$	$S_T > 60$
Long call (X = 60)	0	0	$S_T - 60$
Short call (X = 50)	0	$-(S_T - 50)$	$-(S_T - 50)$
Total	0	$-(S_T - 50)$	-10

Breakeven occurs when the payoff offsets the initial proceeds of $6, which occurs at a stock price of $S_T = \$56$.

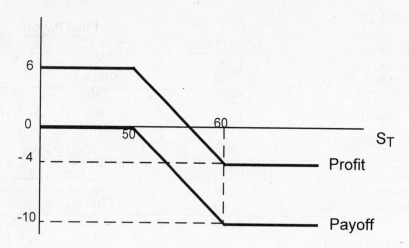

22. Buy a share of stock, write a call with X = 50, write a call with X = 60, and buy a call with X = 110.

Position	$S_T < 50$	$50 < S_T < 60$	$60 < S_T < 110$	$S_T > 110$
Buy stock	S_T	S_T	S_T	S_T
Short call (X = 50)	0	$-(S_T - 50)$	$-(S_T - 50)$	$-(S_T - 50)$
Short call (X = 60)	0	0	$-(S_T - 60)$	$-(S_T - 60)$
Long call (X = 110)	0	0	0	$S_T - 110$
Total	S_T	50	$110 - S_T$	0

The investor is making a volatility bet. Profits will be highest when volatility is low so that the stock price ends up in the interval between $50 and $60.

CHAPTER 15: OPTION VALUATION

1. Put values also increase as the volatility of the underlying stock increases. We see this from the parity relation as follows:

$$C = P + S_0 - PV(X) - PV(Dividends)$$

Given a value of S and a risk-free interest rate, if C increases because of an increase in volatility, so must P to keep the parity equation in balance.

Numerical example:

Suppose you have a put with exercise price 100, and that the stock price can take on one of three values: 90, 100, 110. The payoff to the put for each stock price is:

Stock price	90	100	110
Put value	10	0	0

Now suppose the stock price can take on one of three alternate values also centered around 100, but with less volatility: 95, 100, 105. The payoff to the put for each stock price is:

Stock price	95	100	105
Put value	5	0	0

The payoff to the put in the low volatility example has one-half the expected value of the payoffs in the high volatility example.

2. a. Put A must be written on the lower-priced stock. Otherwise, given the lower volatility of stock A, put A would sell for less than put B.

   b. Put B must be written on the stock with lower price. This would explain its higher value.

   c. Call B. Despite the higher price of stock B, call B is cheaper than call A. This can be explained by a lower time to expiration.

   d. Call B. This would explain its higher price.

   e. Not enough information. The call with the lower exercise price sells for more than the call with the higher exercise price. The values given are consistent with either stock having higher volatility.

3. Note that, as the option becomes progressively more in the money, its hedge ratio increases to a maximum of 1.0:

X	Hedge ratio	X	Hedge ratio
115	85/150 = 0.567	50	150/150 = 1.000
100	100/150 = 0.667	25	150/150 = 1.000
75	125/150 = 0.833	10	150/150 = 1.000

4.

S	d_1	$N(d_1)$
45	-0.0268	0.4893
50	0.5000	0.6915
55	0.9766	0.8356

5. a. When S = 130, then P = 0.

When $S_* = 80$, then P = 30.

The hedge ratio is: $[(P^+ - P^-)/(S^+ - S^-) = [(0 - 30)/(130 - 80)] = -3/5$

b.

Riskless portfolio	S =80	S = 130
3 shares	240	390
5 puts	150	0
Total	390	390

Present value = ($390/1.10) = 354.545

c. Portfolio cost = 3S + 5P = $300 + 5P = $354.545

Therefore 5P = $54.545 $\Rightarrow$ P = $54.545/5 = $10.91

6. The hedge ratio for the call is $[[(C^+ - C^-)/(S^+ - S^-) = [(20 - 0)/(130 - 80)] = 2/5$

Riskless portfolio	S =80	S = 130
2 shares	160	260
Short 5 calls	0	-100
Total	160	160

$-5C + 200 = (160/1.10) = 145.455 \Rightarrow C = 10.91$

Put-call parity relationship: $P = C - S_0 + PV(X)$

$10.91 = 10.91 + (110/1.10) - 100 = 10.91$

7. $d_1 = 0.3182 \quad N(d_1) = 0.6248$

$d_2 = -0.0354 \quad N(d_2) = 0.4859$

$Xe^{-rT} = 47.56$

$C = S_0 N(d_1) - Xe^{-rT} N(d_2) = 8.13$

8. P = 5.69

This value is from our Black-Scholes spreadsheet, but note that we could have derived the value from put-call parity:

$P = C - S_0 + PV(X) = 8.13 - 50 + 47.56 = 5.69$

9. A straddle is a call and a put. The Black-Scholes value is:

$$C + P = S_0 e^{-\delta T} N(d_1) - X e^{-rT} N(d_2) + X e^{-rT} [1 - N(d_2)] - S_0 e^{-\delta T} [1 - N(d_1)]$$

$$= S_0 e^{-\delta T} [2 N(d_1) - 1] + X e^{-rT} [1 - 2N(d_2)]$$

On the Excel spreadsheet (Figure 15.4 in the text), the valuation formula is:

B5*EXP(–B7*B3)*(2*E4 – 1) + B6*EXP(–B4*B3)*(1 – 2*E5)

10. a. C falls to 5.5541
    b. C falls to 4.7911
    c. C falls to 6.0778
    d. C rises to 11.5066
    e. C rises to 8.7187

11. The call price will decrease by less than $1. The change in the call price would be $1 only if: (i) there were a 100% probability that the call would be exercised; and (ii) the interest rate were zero.

12. Holding firm-specific risk constant, higher beta implies higher total stock volatility. Therefore, the value of the put option increases as beta increases.

13. Holding beta constant, the stock with high firm-specific risk has higher total volatility. Therefore, the option on the stock with a lot of firm-specific risk is worth more.

14. The call option with a high exercise price has a lower hedge ratio. The call option is less in the money. Both d_1 and $N(d_1)$ are lower when X is higher.

15. The call option is more sensitive to changes in interest rates. The option elasticity exceeds 1.0. In other words, the option is effectively a levered investment and is more sensitive to interest rate changes.

16. The call option's implied volatility has increased. If this were not the case, then the call price would have fallen.

17. The put option's implied volatility has increased. If this were not the case, then the put price would have fallen.

18. As the stock price becomes infinitely large, the hedge ratio of the call option $[N(d_1)]$ approaches one. As S increases, the probability of exercise approaches 1.0 (i.e., $N(d_1)$ approaches 1.0).

19. The hedge ratio of a put option with a very small exercise price is zero. As X decreases, exercise of the put becomes less and less likely, so the probability of exercise approaches zero. The put's hedge ratio $[N(d_1) -1]$ approaches zero as $N(d_1)$ approaches 1.0.

20. The hedge ratio of the straddle is the sum of the hedge ratios for the two options:
$0.4 + (-0.6) = -0.2$

21. A put is more in the money, and has a hedge ratio closer to –1, when its exercise price is higher:

Put	X	Delta
A	10	-0.1
B	20	-0.5
C	30	-0.9

22. a.

Position	$S_T < X$	$S_T > X$
Stock	$S_T + D$	$S_T + D$
Put	$X - S_T$	0
Total	$X + D$	$S_T + D$

b.

Position	$S_T < X$	$S_T > X$
Call	0	$S_T - X$
Zeroes	$X + D$	$X + D$
Total	$X + D$	$S_T + D$

The total payoffs for each of the two strategies are the same, regardless of the stock price (S_T).

c. The cost of the stock-plus-put portfolio is $(S_0 + P)$. The cost of the call-plus-zero portfolio is: $[C + PV(X + D)]$. Therefore:

$S_0 + P = C + PV(X + D)$

This is the put-call parity relationship in equation 15.3.

23. a. The delta of the collar is calculated as follows:

	Delta
Stock	1.0
Short call	$-N(d_1) = -0.35$
Long put	$N(d_1) - 1 = -0.40$
Total	0.25

If the stock price increases by $1, the value of the collar increases by $0.25. The stock will be worth $1 more, the loss on the short put is $0.40, and the call written is a *liability* that increases by $0.35.

b. If S becomes very large, then the delta of the collar approaches zero. Both $N(d_1)$ terms approach 1 so that the delta for the short call position approaches –1.0 and the delta for the long put position approaches zero. Intuitively, for very large stock prices, the value of the portfolio is simply the (present value of the) exercise price of the call, and is unaffected by small changes in the stock price.

As S approaches zero, the delta of the collar also approaches zero. Both $N(d_1)$ terms approach 0 so that the delta for the short call position approaches zero and the delta for the long put position approaches –1.0. For very small stock prices, the value of the portfolio is simply the (present value of the) exercise price of the put, and is unaffected by small changes in the stock price.

24. a. A. Calls have higher elasticity than shares. For equal *dollar* investments, the capital gain potential for calls is higher than for stocks.

b. B. Calls have hedge ratios less than 1.0. For equal numbers of *shares* controlled, the dollar exposure of the calls is less than that of the stocks, and the profit potential is less.

25. $S_0 = 100$ (current value of portfolio)

$X = 100$ (floor promised to clients, 0% return)

$\sigma = 0.25$ (volatility)

$r = 0.05$ (risk-free rate)

$T = 4$ years (horizon of program)

a. The put delta is: $N(d_1) - 1 = 0.7422 - 1 = -0.2578$

Place 25.78% of the portfolio in bills, 74.22% in equity ($74.22 million)

b. At the new portfolio value, the put delta becomes –0.2779, so that the amount held in bills should be: ($97 million $\times$ 0.2779) = $26.96 million. The manager must sell $1.18 million of equity and use the proceeds to buy bills.

26. a.

Stock price   110   90
Put payoff   0   10

The hedge ratio is –0.5. A portfolio comprised of one share and two puts provides a guaranteed payoff of 110, with present value: (110/1.05) = 104.76 Therefore:

$$S + 2P = 104.76$$
$$100 + 2P = 104.76 \Rightarrow P = 2.38$$

b. The cost of the protective put portfolio is the cost of one share plus the cost of one put: ($100 + $2.38) = $102.38

c. The goal is a portfolio with the same exposure to the stock as the hypothetical protective put portfolio. Since the put's hedge ratio is –0.5, we want to hold (1 – 0.5) = 0.5 shares of stock, which costs $50, and place the remaining funds ($52.38) in bills, earning 5% interest.

Stock price	S = 90	S = 110
Half share	45	55
Bills	55	55
Total	100	110

This payoff is identical to that of the protective put portfolio. Thus, the stock plus bills strategy replicates both the cost and payoff of the protective put.

27. Step 1: Calculate the option values at expiration. The two possible stock prices are: $S^+ = \$120$ and $S^- = \$80$. Therefore, since the exercise price is $100, the corresponding two possible call values are: $C^+ = \$20$ and $C^- = \$0$.

Step 2: Calculate the hedge ratio: $(C^+ - C^-)/(S^+ - S^-) = (20 - 0)/(120 - 80) = 0.5$

Step 3: Form a riskless portfolio made up of one share of stock and two written calls. The cost of the riskless portfolio is: $(S_0 - 2C_0) = 100 - 2C_0$ and the certain end-of-year value is $80.

Step 4: Calculate the present value of $80 with a one-year interest rate of 5% = $76.19

Step 5: Set the value of the hedged position equal to the present value of the certain payoff:

$$\$100 - 2C_0 = \$76.19$$

Step 6: Solve for the value of the call: $C_0 = \$11.90$

Notice that we never use the probabilities of a stock price increase or decrease. These are not needed to value the call option.

28. Step 1: Calculate the option values at expiration. The two possible stock prices are: $S^+ = \$130$ and $S^- = \$70$. Therefore, since the exercise price is $100, the corresponding two possible call values are: $C^+ = \$30$ and $C^- = \$0$.

Step 2: Calculate the hedge ratio: $(C^+ - C^-)/(S^+ - S^-) = (30 - 0)/(130 - 70) = 0.5$

Step 3: Form a riskless portfolio made up of one share of stock and two written calls. The cost of the riskless portfolio is: $(S_0 - 2C_0) = 100 - 2C_0$ and the certain end-of-year value is $70.

Step 4: Calculate the present value of $70 with a one-year interest rate of 5% = $66.67

Step 5: Set the value of the hedged position equal to the present value of the certain payoff:

$$\$100 - 2C_0 = \$66.67$$

Step 6: Solve for the value of the call: $C_0 = \$16.67$

Here, the value of the call is greater than the value of the call in the lower-volatility scenario.

29. We start by finding the value of P^+. From this point, the put can fall to an expiration-date value of $P^{++} = \$0$ (since at this point the stock price is $S^{++} = \$121$) or rise to a final value of $P^{+-} = \$5.50$ (since at this point the stock price is $S^{+-} = \$104.50$, which is less than the $110 exercise price). Therefore, the hedge ratio at this point is:

$$H = \frac{P^{++} - P^{+-}}{S^{++} - S^{+-}} = \frac{\$0 - \$5.50}{\$121 - \$104.50} = -\frac{1}{3}$$

Thus, the following portfolio will be worth $121 at option expiration regardless of the ultimate stock price:

Riskless portfolio	$S^{+-} = \$104.50$	$S^{++} = \$121$
Buy 1 share at price $S^+ = \$110$	$104.50	$121.00
Buy 3 puts at price P^+	16.50	0.00
Total	$121.00	$121.00

The portfolio must have a current market value equal to the present value of $121:

$$110 + 3P^+ = \$121/1.05 = \$115.238 \Rightarrow P^+ = \$1.746$$

Next we find the value of P^-. From this point (at which $S^- = \$95$), the put can fall to an expiration-date value of $P^{-+} = \$5.50$ (since at this point the stock price is $S^{-+} = \$104.50$) or rise to a final value of $P^{--} = \$19.75$ (since at this point, the stock price is $S^{--} = \$90.25$). Therefore, the hedge ratio at this point is -1.0, which reflects the fact that the put will necessarily expire in the money if the stock price falls to $95 in the first period.

$$H = \frac{P^{-+} - P^{--}}{S^{-+} - S^{--}} = \frac{\$5.50 - \$19.75}{\$104.50 - \$90.25} = -1.0$$

Thus, the following portfolio will be worth $110 at option expiration regardless of the ultimate stock price:

Riskless portfolio	$S^{--} = \$90.25$	$S^{-+} = \$104.50$
Buy 1 share at price $S^- = \$95$	$90.25	$104.50
Buy 1 put at price P^-	19.75	5.50
Total	$110.00	$110.00

The portfolio must have a current market value equal to the present value of $110:

$$95 + P^- = \$110/1.05 = \$104.762 \Rightarrow P^- = \$9.762$$

Finally, we solve for P using the values of P^+ and P^-. From its initial value, the put can rise to a value of $P^- = \$9.762$ (at this point the stock price is $S^- = \$95$) or fall to a value of $P^+ = \$1.746$ (at this point, the stock price is $S^+ = \$110$). Therefore, the hedge ratio at this point is:

$$H = \frac{P^+ - P^-}{S^+ - S^-} = \frac{\$1.746 - \$9.762}{\$110 - \$95} = -0.5344$$

Thus, the following portfolio will be worth $60.53 at option expiration regardless of the ultimate stock price:

Riskless portfolio	$S^- = \$95$	$S^+ = \$110$
Buy 0.5344 share at price $S = \$100$	$50.768	$58.784
Buy 1 put at price P	9.762	1.746
Total	$60.530	$60.530

The portfolio must have a market value equal to the present value of $60.53:

$$\$53.44 + P = \$60.53/1.05 = \$57.648 \Rightarrow P = \$4.208$$

Finally, we check put-call parity. Recall from Example 15.1 and Concept Check #4 that C = $4.434. Put-call parity requires that:

$$P = C + PV(X) - S$$

$$\$4.208 = \$4.434 + (\$110/1.05^2) - \$100$$

Except for minor rounding error, put-call parity is satisfied.

CHAPTER 16: FUTURES MARKETS

1. a.

2. d.

3. Total losses may amount to $525 before a margin call is received. Each contract calls for delivery of 5,000 ounces. Before a margin call is received, the price per ounce can increase by: ($525/5,000 = $0.105 (or $0.11, given that prices are quoted only to the penny). The futures price at this point would be ($8 + $0.11) = $8.11

4. a. The closing price for the spot index was 1,146.19. The dollar value of stocks is thus: ($250 × 1,146.19) = $286,547.50
        The closing futures price for the March contract was 1,149.00, which has a dollar value of: (1,149.00 × $250) = $287,250
        Therefore, the required margin is $28,725.

    b. The futures price increases by (1,200 − 1,149) = 51. The credit to your margin account would be (51 × $250) = $12,750, which is a percent gain of: ($12,750/$28,725) = 44.4%. Note that the futures price itself increased by only 4.44%.

    c. Following the reasoning in part (b), any change in F is magnified by a ratio of [1/(margin requirement)]. This is the leverage effect. The return will be −10%.

5. There is little hedging demand for cement futures because cement prices are relatively stable and, even in construction, cement is a small part of total costs. There is little speculative demand for cement futures because since cement prices are fairly stable and predictable so that there is little opportunity to profit from price changes.

6. The ability to buy on margin is one advantage of futures. Another is the ease with which one can alter holdings of the asset. This is especially important if one is dealing in commodities, for which the futures market is far more liquid than the spot market so that transaction costs are lower in the futures market.

7. Short selling results in an immediate cash inflow, whereas the short futures position does not:

Action	Initial Cash Flow	Cash Flow at Time T
Short sale	$+P_0$	$-P_T$
Short futures	0	$F_0 - P_T$

8. a.

Action	Initial Cash Flow	Cash Flow at Time T
Buy stock	$-S_0$	$S_T + D$
Short futures	0	$F_0 - S_T$
Borrow	S_0	$-S_0(1 + r)$
Total	0	$F_0 + D - S_0(1 + r)$

b. The net initial investment is zero, whereas the final cash flow is not zero. Therefore to avoid arbitrage opportunities the equilibrium futures price will be the final cash flow equated to zero. Accordingly: $F_0 = S_0(1 + r) - D$

c. Noting that $D = (d \times S_0)$, we substitute and rearrange to find that:
$F_0 = S_0 (1 + r - d)$

9. a. $F_0 = S_0(1 + r_f) = \$150 \times 1.06 = \$159.00$

b. $F_0 = S_0(1 + r_f)^3 = \$150 \times (1.06)^3 = \$178.65$

c. $F_0 = S_0(1 + r_f)^3 = \$150 \times (1.08)^3 = \$188.96$

10. As S increases, so will F. You should buy the futures. A long position in futures is better than buying the stock since you get the advantage of buying on margin.

11. a. Take a short position in T-bond futures, to offset interest rate risk. If rates increase, the loss on the bond will be offset by gains on the futures.

b. Again, a short position in T-bond futures will offset the bond price risk.

c. You wish to protect your cash outlay when the bond is purchased. If bond prices increase you will need extra cash to purchase the bond with the anticipated contribution. Thus, you want a long futures position that will generate a profit if prices increase.

12. $F_0 = S_0(1 + r_f - d) = 1300 \times (1 + 0.05 - 0.02) = 1339$

13. According to the parity relationship, the proper price for December futures is:

$F_{Dec} = F_{June} \times (1 + r_f)^{1/2} = 346.30 \times (1.05)^{1/2} = 354.85$

The actual futures price for December is too high relative to the June price. You should short the December contract and long the June contract.

14.　a.　$F_0 = S_0(1 + r_f) = 120 \times 1.06 = 127.20$

　　b.　The stock price falls to: $[\$120 \times (1 - 0.03)] = \$116.40$

　　　　The futures price falls to: $(\$116.40 \times 1.06) = \$123.384$

　　　　The investor loses $(\$127.20 - \$123.384) \times 1{,}000 = \$3816.00$

　　c.　The percentage return is: $(-\$3{,}816/\$12{,}000) = -31.8\%$

15.　a.　The initial futures price is:

$$F_0 = 1{,}200 \times (1 + 0.005 - 0.002)^{12} = 1{,}243.92$$

　　　In one month, the futures price will be:

$$F_0 = 1{,}210 \times (1 + 0.005 - 0.002)^{11} = 1{,}250.53$$

　　　The increase in the futures price is 6.61, so the cash flow will be:

$$(6.61 \times \$250) = \$1{,}652.50$$

　　b.　The holding period return is: $(\$1{,}652.50/\$15{,}000) = 0.110 = 11.0\%$

16.　The important distinction between a futures contract and an options contract is that the futures contract is an obligation. When an investor purchases or sells a futures contract, the investor has an obligation to accept or deliver, respectively, the underlying commodity on the delivery date. In contrast, the buyer of an option contract is not obligated to accept or deliver the underlying commodity but instead has the right, or choice, to accept or deliver the underlying commodity anytime during the life of the contract.

　　Futures and options modify a portfolio's risk in different ways. Buying or selling a futures contract affects a portfolio's upside risk and downside risk by a similar magnitude. This is commonly referred to as symmetrical impact. On the other hand, the addition of a call or put option to a portfolio does not affect a portfolio's upside risk and downside risk to a similar magnitude. Unlike futures contracts, the impact of options on the risk profile of a portfolio is asymmetrical.

17.　The parity value of F_0 is: $1{,}200 \times (1 + 0.05 - 0.02) = 1{,}236$. The actual futures price is 1,243, overpriced by 7.

Action	Initial Cash Flow	Cash Flow at Time T (one year)
Buy index	-1200	$S_T + (0.02 \times 1{,}200)$ [CF includes 2% dividend]
Short futures	0	$1243 - S_T$
Borrow	1200	-1200×1.05
Total	0	7 [A riskless cash flow]

18. a. The current yield on the bonds (coupon divided by price) plays the role of the dividend yield.

b. When the yield curve is upward sloping, the current yield exceeds the short-term interest rate. Hence, net cost of carry is negative, and distant futures prices will be lower than near-term futures prices.

c. In Figure 16.2, the longer-term (June) T-bond contracts do in fact sell at lower prices than near-term (March) contracts.

19. a. From parity: $F_0 = [400 \times (1 + 0.03)] - 5 = 407$. Actual F_0 is 406, so the futures price is \$1 below its "proper" or parity value.

b. Buy the relatively cheap futures and sell the relatively expensive stock.

Action	Initial Cash Flow	Cash Flow at Time T
Sell stock	+400	$-(S_T + 5)$
Buy futures	0	$S_T - 406$
Lend \$400	-400	+412
Total	0	1

c. If you do not receive interest on the proceeds of the short sales, then the \$400 you receive will not be invested, but rather will simply be returned to you. The proceeds from the strategy in part (b) is now negative: an arbitrage opportunity no longer exists.

Action	Initial Cash Flow	Cash Flow at Time T
Sell stock	+400	$-(S_T + 5)$
Buy futures	0	$S_T - 406$
Place \$400 in margin account	-400	+400
Total	0	-11

d. If we call the original futures price F_0, then the proceeds from the long-futures, short-stock strategy are:

Action	Initial Cash Flow	Cash Flow at Time T
Sell stock	+400	$-(S_T + 5)$
Buy futures	0	$S_T - F_0$
Place \$400 in margin account	-400	+400
Total	0	$395 - F_0$

Therefore, F_0 can be as low as 395 without giving rise to an arbitrage opportunity. On the other hand, if F_0 is higher than the parity value (407) an arbitrage opportunity (buy stocks, sell futures) will open up. There is no short-selling cost in this case. Therefore, the no-arbitrage region is:

$$395 \leq F_0 \leq 407$$

20.   a.   Each contract is for $250 times the index, currently valued at 1400. Therefore, each contract has the same exposure to the market as $350,000 worth of stock, and to hedge a $7 million portfolio, you need: $7 million/$350,000 = 20 contracts

      b.   The parity value of the futures price = $1400 \times (1 + 0.02 - 0.01) = 1414'$

Action	Initial Cash Flow	Cash Flow at Time T
Short 20 futures contracts	0	$20 \times 250 \times (1414 - S_T)$
Buy 5,000 "shares" of index (each share equals $1,400)	-$7 million	($7 million $\times$ 0.01) + (5,000 $\times$ S_T)
Total	0	$7.14 million [which is riskless]

Thus the riskless return on the hedged strategy equals the T-bill rate of 2%.

      c.   Now, your stock swings only 0.6 as much as the market index. Hence, you need 0.6 as many contracts as in part (a): $(0.60 \times 20) = 12$ contracts. In this case, however, the hedged position will not be riskless since you are exposed to the stock's unsystematic risk. The beta of the hedged position is zero since all the systematic risk is hedged.

21.   The dollar value of the index is thus: $(\$250 \times 1200) = \$300,000$ and therefore requires a margin of $30,000.

If the futures price decreases by 1% to 1188 the decline in the futures price is 12. The decrease in your margin account would be: $(12 \times \$250) = \$3,000$. This is a percent return of: $(-\$3,000/\$30,000) = -10\%$. Cash in the margin account is now: $(\$30,000 - \$3,000) = \$27,000$.

22.   a.   The initial futures price is: $F_0 = 400 \times (1 + 0.005 - 0.002)^{12} = 414.640$

In one month, the maturity of the contract will be only 11 months, so the futures price will be: $F_0 = 410 \times (1 + 0.005 - 0.002)^{11} = 423.735$

The increase in the futures price is 9.095, so the cash flow will be:

$9.095 \times \$500 = \$4,547.50$

      b.   The holding period return is: $(\$4,547.50/\$15,000) = 0.303 = 30.3\%$

23.   The Treasurer would like to buy the bonds today, but cannot. As a proxy for this purchase, T-bond futures contracts can be purchased. If rates do in fact fall, the Treasurer will have to buy back the bonds for the sinking fund at prices higher than the prices at which they could be purchased today. However, the gains on the futures contracts will offset this higher cost.

CHAPTER 17: INVESTORS AND THE INVESTMENT PROCESS

1.   b.   Purchasing power risk.

2.   b.   Organizing the management process itself.

3.   d.   All investors.

4.   b.   The level of the market.

5.   a.   Paying benefits to retired employees.

6.   c.   Determines most of the portfolio's returns and volatility over time.

7.   *Investor Objectives:*
Return Requirements. Often, the return is stated in terms of minimum levels required to fund a specific liability or budget requirements as indicated by the Wood Museum Treasurer. The minimum returns to meet the budget requirements are: 1998 -- 12%; 1999 -- 13%; and 2000 -- 14%. The trustees have to clarify how capital gains should be treated relative to the budget.

Risk Tolerance – the client's willingness or ability to bear risk in the pursuit of specified return requirements. For Wood Museum, the tight budget position and the trustees' fears of a financial crisis indicate a low tolerance for risk.

Investor Constraints:
Liquidity Requirements – the client's need for cash or cash availability from securities that can be sold quickly and without substantial price risk (concessions). Wood Museum's liquidity needs are a significant factor given the budget considerations.

Time Horizon – the client's expected holding period, which is generally determined by such factors as the nature of the client's liabilities, cash flow requirements or expectations. Investment managers also have an expectational time horizon, which is the distance into the future that the manager feels he can predict important financial variables, such as earnings and dividends, with reasonable accuracy. For Wood Museum, the immediacy of the budget requirements (1 to 3 years) suggests a very short time horizon for at least a major portion of the portfolio.

Tax Considerations – Wood Museum is tax exempt.

Regulatory and Legal Considerations – In the case of an endowment fund, prudent-man factors must be considered as well as the legal structure of the fund and any state or federal regulation that might influence the management of the investment portfolio.

Unique Needs and Circumstances – particular conditions or requirements that reflect the discretion of the fund trustees. For example, social factors might be a concern of the Museum that the trustees want reflected in the types of investment

8.   The most important area of change concerns taxes. Mrs. Atkins pays income tax, but the endowment fund will be free of taxes.

OBJECTIVES

Return Requirement: The fund should strive to provide a predictable stream of income growing in line with inflation. An initial income target of 5% of portfolio assets should enable the fund to support the hospital's operating budget, while still favoring future growth.

Risk Tolerance: In view of the relatively long time horizon, limited liquidity needs, and adequacy of already existing endowment assets to offset the operating deficit, the Atkins Fund has an above average ability to assume risk.

CONSTRAINTS

Liquidity: Liquidity needs are low. Except for investment reasons and periodic payment of accumulated income, there is no reason to maintain any sizable liquid reserves in the fund.

Time Horizon: Endowment funds typically have very long time horizons and there is no reason to believe that the current case is any exception. Certainly the time horizon extends well beyond normal market cycles.

Tax Considerations: Since endowment funds are normally free from taxes, with the exception of minimal estate taxes, taxes would not be a meaningful constraint for this fund.

Legal: Most endowment funds are governed by state regulations, and since most states have moved to a "prudent man" standard, regulatory and legal constraints should not be significant investment factors (certainly no more so than during the time that Mrs. Atkins is alive).

Unique Needs: Although the details provided concerning Good Samaritan are somewhat sketchy, and additional information might be appropriately requested, it would appear that this hospital is experiencing financial difficulties which have been characteristic of this industry for several years. The existence of an operating deficit, and the possibility that this deficit may grow, suggest that a slightly more conservative posture relative to other endowment funds might be appropriate.

9. a. An appropriate investment policy statement for the endowment fund will be organized around the following major, specific aspects of the situation:
    1. The primacy of the current income requirement;
    2. The inability to accept significant risk as to 85% of the original capital;
    3. The 10-year time horizon that exists within the fund's infinite life span;
    4. The unique and dominating circumstance represented by the June 30, 2006, capital payout requirement; and
    5. The requirements of the "spending rule."

    A proposed statement might be:
    "The endowment fund's investment assets shall be managed in a Prudent Man context to provide a total return of at least 8% per year, including an original $500,000 (5%) current income component growing at 3% annually. Meeting this current income goal is the primary return objective. Inasmuch as $8,500,000 of capital must be distributed in cash on June 30, 2006, no significant risk can be taken on the sum that is required to guarantee this payout; a normal risk capacity shall be assumed with respect to remaining investment assets. The fund's horizon is very long term as to assets not required for the 2006 distribution. The endowment fund 'spending rule' shall be taken into account in determining investment strategy and annual income distributions."

    b. The account circumstances will affect the initial asset allocation in the following major ways:
    1. The aggregate portfolio will have much larger than normal holdings of U.S. Treasury and Treasury-related securities. Maximum use will be made of discount Treasuries and related zero-coupon securities in order to minimize the risk and the amount of total assets that must be "frozen" in order to assure the availability of $8,500,000 on June 30, 2006.
    2. The aggregate portfolio will have much smaller than normal holdings of equity securities, given the need to "lock up" the 2006 distribution requirement in virtually riskless form. The initial mix here might well be 15% zeros, 55% discount Treasuries, and only 30% equities; normally, 60 to 70% in equities would not be uncommon.
    3. The equity portfolio will emphasize a growth orientation. Income in excess of the current income requirement will be added to equity. Not only must building of future value and income be derived from the rather small equity component of the portfolio, but it must also serve an inflation protection need as well. Since it does not appear that meeting the annual current income target will be difficult initially, there is plenty of room for lower yielding issues to be included in the equity mix.
    4. The aggregate portfolio risk level will be well below average. The 2006 payout requirement dictates a zero risk posture on a large part of the total while the prudent man environment will act to prevent overzealous risk taking in the "remainder" portion.
    5. The fund's tax-exempt status maximizes allocation flexibility, both as to income aspects and as to planning for future capital growth.
    6. A ten-year horizon must be accommodated as to a major portion of total capital funds, while a very long-term horizon applies to the rest.

10. a. Investment *objectives* are goals; *constraints* are the limits within which the responsible party must operate in order to achieve the objectives; *policies* define the ways in which the effort to achieve the objectives will be undertaken.

The primary function of an *investment objective* is to identify the risk/return relationship sought for an account. Emphasis may be on minimizing return while accepting an appropriate level of risk. Objectives may be specified in either absolute or relative form. For example:
    "8% total return while experiencing a risk level equivalent to the S&P 500" or,
    "a target total return of 3% per annum greater than the rate of inflation with a standard deviation no greater than that of the S&P 500 in the post World War II period"

An i*nvestment constraint* is a limitation on the investment decision-making which can be identified as a requirement in terms of liquidity, time horizon, tax considerations, legal or regulatory considerations and unique needs. The realism of both the investment objectives and the practical policies adopted for managing the account must be tested against any investment constraints. For example: an investment advisor to an ERISA plan is legally constrained by virtue of inclusion as a fiduciary under the law, and cannot purchase for the plan portfolio more than 10% of the common stock of the plan sponsor.

An i*nvestment policy* is an operational statement or guideline that specifies the actions to be taken in order to achieve the investment objective within the constraints imposed.

b. **OBJECTIVES**
Return: Total return equal to or greater than the foundation's annual spending plus the rate of inflation in medical school tuition.
Risk Tolerance: Moderate – no less volatility than long-term bonds and no more volatility than a diversified portfolio of common stocks.

CONSTRAINTS
Time Horizon: Long-term (perpetuity).
Liquidity: Modest percentage (5% to 10%) of assets must be available for annual distribution.
Legal and Regulatory: State regulation and/or the endowment documents.
Taxes: none.

c. **INVESTMENT POLICIES**

A portfolio balance, to be averaged over time, of a maximum position of 67% in equity-type investments and a minimum position of 33% in fixed income type investments.

Qualified equity and fixed income investments to consist of the following:

Equity Related	Fixed Income
Common stocks and warrants	Government and agency obligations
Convertible securities	Corporate obligations
Option writing	Real estate mortgages

In the case of convertible securities, corporate obligations and preferred stocks carrying a credit rating, qualifying for purchase are securities rated no less than BBB ("regarded as having an adequate capacity to pay interest / dividends and repay principal") as defined by S&P, or its equivalent, as defined by other recognized rating agencies. Stocks to be of high quality with betas not to exceed 1.2 for portfolio as a whole.

The Office of the Treasurer to have direct responsibility for no more than 50% of total marketable endowment funds. Remaining funds to be the responsibility of outside managers as selected from time to time. All managers to have full investment discretion within defined statements of objectives and policies.

As a charitable foundation, must distribute minimum of 5% of assets annually in order to avoid loss of tax-exempt status.

Sufficient funds available for annual disbursement. Money market instruments rated A-1 may be utilized for a liquidity reserve.

11. The investment objectives of the Masons should be expressed in terms of return and risk. These return and risk preferences should be portrayed in terms of the Mason's preferences, their current financial status, and the stage in their life cycle.

The objectives of the portfolio are:

Return Requirement: Dr. Mason is nearing retirement. Therefore, the overriding objective is to provide the Masons with sufficient retirement income. This objective should be easily satisfied by investing the original $1,000,000 payment from ACS to provide a moderate current income level. This income, combined with the Masons' Social Security and pension benefits, will provide sufficient retirement income. Because of the large cash payment from ACS (even after payment of capital gains taxes), the Masons will have a large enough financial base to pursue their other objectives, specifically, for the grandchildren and for scholarships to the Essex Institute. These latter two objectives suggest a portfolio seeking long-term capital appreciation. Therefore, the substantial size of the assets permits a growth-oriented posture with a secondary emphasis on current income. Common stocks and equity real estate provide growth opportunities, and the latter may also provide tax benefits.

Risk Tolerance: Given the substantial size of the Masons' assets, this portfolio can tolerate a larger amount of risk than is normal for a family in the later stage of their life cycle. Coupled with the Masons' retirement benefits, a moderate income from the portfolio will provide sufficient retirement income. Therefore, the portfolio can accept greater risk in the pursuit of higher long-term capital appreciation. A significant portion of the Masons' assets can be invested in growth assets, such as common stocks and real estate, with secondary emphasis on investments with a high current income yield. The greater the amount of royalties received, the greater the risk-tolerance for the portfolio.

The constraints on the achievement of the portfolio objectives are:

Liquidity: The substantial size of the Masons' assets and the prospects for continued high royalty income lessen the importance of the liquidity constraint. A major portion of the portfolio should be invested in relatively non-liquid assets in order to achieve long-term capital growth.

Time Horizon: Because the Masons are in the later part of their life cycle, one would ordinarily expect them to have a relatively short time horizon. The size of the Masons' assets, however, and the objectives of providing for the education of their grandchildren and for scholarships, dictate that a substantial portion of the portfolio be invested for the longer term. Common stocks and real estate would be appropriate.

Regulatory and Legal: Since this is a personal portfolio, regulatory and legal constraints are not important.

Tax Considerations: The income from royalties and investments will require that the portfolio be structured for favorable tax treatment. Long-term growth assets, which enjoy deferral of gains until the sale of the assets, are suitable. Real estate, in the form of rental property, provides tax deductions that might also be desirable, and rental income would supplement common stock dividends to provide the moderate current income required.

Investment Policy: Given the Masons' substantial assets, the investment policy should emphasize capital appreciation and provide moderate current income. The large size of the portfolio allows the purchase of growth-oriented common stocks while providing sufficient retirement income. This policy will provide the opportunity to achieve the objectives of educating the grandchildren and funding the scholarships to the Essex Institute, while providing enough retirement income. Growth assets should also be a better inflation hedge. Real estate, tax-exempt bonds, and low-risk money market investments would provide the necessary diversification.

12. a. Mature pension fund:
    Return requirement: Return must exceed the fund's actuarially assumed rate of return based in part on the anticipated 9% rate for wage cost increases.
    Risk tolerance: Proximity of payouts limits tolerance for risk taking. As a result, the portfolio's asset mix should lean toward intermediate-maturity fixed-income assets of relatively high quality.
    Liquidity: Proximity of payouts requires liquidity above that required for less mature plans. This additional liquidity may limit returns.
    Time horizon: Again, maturity of plan results in an emphasis on short- to intermediate-term time horizon that may limit returns.
    Tax considerations: Non-taxable.
    Regulatory and legal: Federal (U.S.-ERISA) and state laws will affect asset mix and quality.

   b. Conservative endowment fund:
    Return requirement: Return must meet or exceed 5% spending rate plus 8% inflation rate. Return can be from income or capital gains but budget requirements would place the emphasis on income. Inflation considerations require some consideration of long-term growth.
    Risk tolerance: With a 13% return objective, some risk tolerance may be required but the certainty of return will temper this risk tolerance.
    Liquidity: Budget needs will require some liquidity to meet expenses; this may limit returns.
    Time horizon: Budget considerations will require funding immediate needs but inflation considerations require some attention to a longer-term growth horizon.
    Tax considerations: Non-taxable.
    Regulatory and legal: State regulation.

    It would also be important to recognize the dichotomy of objectives of the endowment fund: maximizing assured returns to fund current needs over a short-term time horizon, and maximizing more risky returns to maintain long-term real value of the endowment's principal value over a long-term time horizon.

   c. Life insurance company specializing in annuities:
    Return requirement: Return should exceed new money rate by sufficient margin to meet expenses and profit objectives. Lower minimum accumulation rate tempers return objective.
    Risk tolerance: With a 14% new money return objective, some risk tolerance may be required, but certainty of return and avoidance of reinvestment rate risk virtually mandates the use of an immunized fixed income portfolio.
    Liquidity: Some liquidity may be required for surrenders and rollover of funds to protect against locking in noncompetitive rates.
    Time horizon: Shorter than normal time horizon because annuities are subject to disintermediation.
    Tax considerations: A minor factor because competition will require a high rate of return, most of which will accumulate for the policyholder and thus not be subject to tax.
    Regulatory and legal: Significant state regulation will affect asset mix and quality.

CHAPTER 18: TAXES, INFLATION,
AND INVESTMENT STRATEGY

1. With a savings rate of 16%, the retirement annuity would be $205,060 (compared to $192,244 with the 15% savings rate).

Spreadsheet 18.1: Adjusted for Change in Savings Rate

	A	B	C	D	E
1	Retirement Years	Income growth	Savings rate	ROR	
2	**25**	**0.07**	**0.16**	**0.06**	
3	Age	Income	Saving	Cumulative Savings	Consumption
4	30	50,000	8,000	8,000	42,000
5	31	53,500	8,560	17,040	44,940
6	32	57,245	9,159	27,222	48,086
9	35	70,128	11,220	65,769	58,907
19	45	137,952	22,072	329,450	115,879
29	55	271,372	43,419	1,006,376	227,952
39	65	533,829	85,413	2,621,352	448,416
40	**Total**	**7,445,673**	**1,191,308**	**Retirement Annuity**	**205,060**

2. With a savings rate of 16%, the retirement annuity will be $52,979 (vs. $49,668). The growth in the real retirement annuity (6.67%) is the same as with the case of no inflation.

Spreadsheet 18.2: Adjusted for Change in Savings Rate

	A	B	C	D	E	F
1	Retirement Years	Income growth	Rate of Inflation	Savings rate	ROR	rROR
2	**25**	**0.07**	**0.03**	**0.16**	**0.06**	**0.0291**
3	Age	Income	Deflator	Saving	Cumulative Savings	rConsumption
4	30	50,000	1.00	8,000	8,000	42,000
5	31	53,500	1.03	8,560	17,040	43,631
9	35	70,128	1.16	11,220	65,769	50,814
19	45	137,952	1.56	22,072	329,450	74,379
29	55	271,372	2.09	43,419	1,006,376	108,871
39	65	533,829	2.81	85,413	2,621,352	159,360
40	**Total**	**7,445,673**		**1,191,308**	**Real Annuity**	**52,979**

3. The objective is to obtain a real retirement annuity of $49,668, as in Spreadsheet 18.2. In Spreadsheet 18.3: Saving from Real Income, add cell F42 for the desired annuity and cell F43 for the difference between the annuity with savings from real income and the desired annuity in cell E42. Select Tools/Solver from the menu bar. Set up solver parameters as in the picture below the adjusted Spreadsheet 18.3.

Spreadsheet 18.3: With Target Cell for Desired Real Annuity

	A	B	C	D	E	F
1	Retirement Years	Income growth	Savings rate	ROR	Rate of Inflation	rROR
2	25	0.07	0.100	0.06	0.03	0.0291
3	Age	Income	Saving	Cumulative Savings	Deflator	rConsumption
4	30	50,000	5,000	5,000	1.00	45,000
5	31	53,500	5,511	10,811	1.03	46,592
6	32	57,245	6,073	17,532	1.06	48,234
7	33	61,252	6,693	25,277	1.09	49,929
8	34	65,540	7,377	34,171	1.13	51,677
9	35	70,128	8,130	44,351	1.16	53,480
10	36	75,037	8,960	55,971	1.19	55,338
11	37	80,289	9,875	69,204	1.23	57,253
12	38	85,909	10,883	84,239	1.27	59,227
13	39	91,923	11,994	101,287	1.30	61,259
14	40	98,358	13,218	120,583	1.34	63,352
15	41	105,243	14,568	142,386	1.38	65,505
16	42	112,610	16,055	166,985	1.43	67,721
17	43	120,492	17,695	194,698	1.47	70,000
18	44	128,927	19,501	225,882	1.51	72,343
19	45	137,952	21,492	260,927	1.56	74,751
20	46	147,608	23,687	300,269	1.60	77,224
21	47	157,941	26,105	344,391	1.65	79,763
22	48	168,997	28,771	393,825	1.70	82,368
23	49	180,826	31,708	449,162	1.75	85,040
24	50	193,484	34,945	511,057	1.81	87,779
25	51	207,028	38,513	580,234	1.86	90,585
26	52	221,520	42,446	657,494	1.92	93,458
27	53	237,026	46,779	743,722	1.97	96,397
28	54	253,618	51,555	839,901	2.03	99,402
29	55	271,372	56,819	947,114	2.09	102,471
30	56	290,368	62,620	1,066,562	2.16	105,605
31	57	310,693	69,014	1,199,569	2.22	108,801
32	58	332,442	76,060	1,347,604	2.29	112,058
33	59	355,713	83,826	1,512,286	2.36	115,374
34	60	380,613	92,385	1,695,408	2.43	118,746
35	61	407,256	101,817	1,898,950	2.50	122,171
36	62	435,764	112,213	2,125,099	2.58	125,647
37	63	466,267	123,670	2,376,275	2.65	129,168
38	64	498,906	136,296	2,655,148	2.73	132,731
39	65	533,829	150,212	2,964,669	2.81	136,331
40		Dollars saved	1,572,466		Real Annuity	59,918
41						
42					Real annuity-Nominal savings	49,668
43					target cell(=F40-F42)	10,250

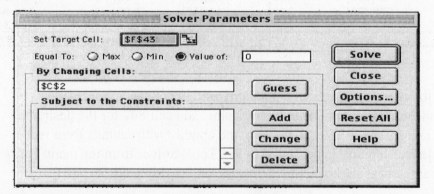

We find that a savings rate of 8.3% (C2) from real income yields the desired real retirement annuity, as the modified spreadsheet below shows.

	A	B	C	D	E	F
1	Retirement Years	Income growth	Savings rate	ROR	Rate of Inflation	rROR
2	25	0.07	0.083	0.06	0.03	0.0291
3	Age	Income	Saving	Cumulative Savings	Deflator	rConsumption
4	30	50,000	4,145	4,145	1.00	45,855
5	31	53,500	4,568	8,961	1.03	47,507
6	32	57,245	5,034	14,533	1.06	49,214
7	33	61,252	5,548	20,953	1.09	50,977
8	34	65,540	6,115	28,325	1.13	52,798
9	35	70,128	6,739	36,764	1.16	54,680
10	36	75,037	7,427	46,397	1.19	56,622
11	37	80,289	8,185	57,366	1.23	58,627
12	38	85,909	9,021	69,829	1.27	60,696
13	39	91,923	9,942	83,961	1.30	62,831
14	40	98,358	10,957	99,955	1.34	65,034
15	41	105,243	12,076	118,029	1.38	67,306
16	42	112,610	13,309	138,419	1.43	69,647
17	43	120,492	14,668	161,392	1.47	72,061
18	44	128,927	16,165	187,241	1.51	74,549
19	45	137,952	17,816	216,291	1.56	77,111
20	46	147,608	19,635	248,904	1.60	79,749
21	47	157,941	21,640	285,477	1.65	82,464
22	48	168,997	23,849	326,455	1.70	85,259
23	49	180,826	26,284	372,326	1.75	88,133
24	50	193,484	28,967	423,633	1.81	91,089
25	51	207,028	31,925	480,976	1.86	94,127
26	52	221,520	35,185	545,019	1.92	97,247
27	53	237,026	38,777	616,498	1.97	100,451
28	54	253,618	42,736	696,223	2.03	103,740
29	55	271,372	47,099	785,096	2.09	107,114
30	56	290,368	51,908	884,110	2.16	110,572
31	57	310,693	57,208	994,365	2.22	114,116
32	58	332,442	63,049	1,117,076	2.29	117,745
33	59	355,713	69,486	1,253,587	2.36	121,459
34	60	380,613	76,581	1,405,383	2.43	125,257
35	61	407,256	84,400	1,574,106	2.50	129,138
36	62	435,764	93,017	1,761,569	2.58	133,101
37	63	466,267	102,514	1,969,777	2.65	137,144
38	64	498,906	112,981	2,200,945	2.73	141,266
39	65	533,829	124,516	2,457,518	2.81	145,463
40		Dollars saved	1,303,472		Real Annuity	49,668
41						
42					Real annuity-Nominal savings	49,668
43					target cell(=F40-F42)	0

4. No, for two reasons.
   1. Because of the exemption from taxable income, only part of income is subject to tax, while ROR affects all savings.
   2. Increases in savings resulting from an increase in ROR compound over time.

A 1% increase in the tax rate, from 25% to 26% (all else equal), reduces the real annuity from $37,882 to $37,426. A 1% increase in ROR, from 6% to 7%, increases the real annuity from $37,882 to $49,107. Making both changes simultaneously yields a real annuity of $48,505.

5. In the original Spreadsheet 18.5, real consumption during retirement is $60,789. A 1% increase in the rate of inflation will reduce real consumption during retirement to $15,780.

A 1% increase in the flat-tax rate will reduce real consumption during retirement to $58,983.

The root of the difference is similar to that of the case of ROR compared to tax rates (see problem 4). While the tax rate affects only part of the income, an increase in the rate of inflation affects all savings, and the reduction in real savings compound over time.

Note that, in this example, real consumption during the saving period is fixed, set to equal consumption in Spreadsheet 18.4. To sustain this level of real consumption with a 4% inflation rate, investors must withdraw funds from the saving account as of age 60. In reality, however, households reduce consumption in the face of deteriorating circumstances in order to protect the retirement annuity.

Spreadsheet 18.5: Adjusted for Higher Rate of Inflation

	A	B	C	D	E	F	G	H
1	Retirement Years	Income growth	Rate of Inflation	Exemption now	Tax Rate	Saving rate	ROR	rROR
2	25	0.07	0.04	15000	0.25	0.15	0.06	0.0192
3	Age	Income	Deflator	Exemption	Taxes	Savings	Cumulative Savings	rConsumption
4	30	50,000	1.00	15,000	5,016	9,922	9,922	35,063
5	31	53,500	1.04	15,600	5,518	10,309	20,826	36,224
6	32	57,245	1.08	16,224	6,065	10,698	32,774	37,428
7	33	61,252	1.12	16,873	6,659	11,086	45,826	38,678
8	34	65,540	1.17	17,548	7,304	11,472	60,048	39,974
9	35	70,128	1.22	18,250	8,005	11,852	75,503	41,319
10	36	75,037	1.27	18,980	8,767	12,224	92,257	42,713
11	37	80,289	1.32	19,739	9,593	12,584	110,376	44,160
12	38	85,909	1.37	20,529	10,490	12,928	129,927	45,661
13	39	91,923	1.42	21,350	11,464	13,253	150,976	47,218
14	40	98,358	1.48	22,204	12,521	13,551	173,586	48,834
15	41	105,243	1.54	23,092	13,666	13,819	197,820	50,509
16	42	112,610	1.60	24,015	14,909	14,050	223,739	52,248
17	43	120,492	1.67	24,976	16,256	14,236	251,400	54,052
18	44	128,927	1.73	25,975	17,716	14,370	280,854	55,923
19	45	137,952	1.80	27,014	19,299	14,442	312,148	57,864
20	46	147,608	1.87	28,095	21,014	14,443	345,320	59,878
21	47	157,941	1.95	29,219	22,872	14,361	380,400	61,968
22	48	168,997	2.03	30,387	24,885	14,183	417,407	64,136
23	49	180,826	2.11	31,603	27,065	13,896	456,348	66,386
24	50	193,484	2.19	32,867	29,427	13,484	497,213	68,720
25	51	207,028	2.28	34,182	31,983	12,930	539,976	71,141
26	52	221,520	2.37	35,549	34,751	12,215	584,590	73,654
27	53	237,026	2.46	36,971	37,748	11,317	630,982	76,261
28	54	253,618	2.56	38,450	40,991	10,213	679,054	78,966
29	55	271,372	2.67	39,988	44,501	8,877	728,674	81,773
30	56	290,368	2.77	41,587	48,300	7,280	779,674	84,685
31	57	310,693	2.88	43,251	52,411	5,390	831,845	87,707
32	58	332,442	3.00	44,981	56,858	3,172	884,927	90,843
33	59	355,713	3.12	46,780	61,669	587	938,610	94,097
34	60	380,613	3.24	48,651	66,874	-2,408	992,519	97,474
35	61	407,256	3.37	50,597	72,504	-5,859	1,046,211	100,978
36	62	435,764	3.51	52,621	78,592	-9,819	1,099,164	104,614
37	63	466,267	3.65	54,726	85,177	-14,346	1,150,768	108,387
38	64	498,906	3.79	56,915	92,299	-19,502	1,200,312	112,302
39	65	533,829	3.95	59,191	99,999	-25,356	1,246,974	116,365
40	Total			1,163,975	1,203,168	265,856	Real Annuity	16,040
41	RETIREMENT							
42	Age	Nom Withdraw	Deflator	Exemption	Taxes		Fund left	rConsumption
43	66	65,827	4.10	61,559	1,067		1,255,966	15,780
44	67	68,460	4.27	64,021	1,110		1,262,864	15,780
45	68	71,199	4.44	66,582	1,154		1,267,437	15,780
46	69	74,046	4.62	69,245	1,200		1,269,437	15,780
47	70	77,008	4.80	72,015	1,248		1,268,594	15,780
48	71	80,089	4.99	74,896	1,298		1,264,621	15,780
49	72	83,292	5.19	77,892	1,350		1,257,206	15,780
50	73	86,624	5.40	81,007	1,404		1,246,015	15,780
51	74	90,089	5.62	84,248	1,460		1,230,687	15,780
52	75	93,692	5.84	87,618	1,519		1,210,836	15,780
53	76	97,440	6.07	91,122	1,579		1,186,046	15,780
54	77	101,338	6.32	94,767	1,643		1,155,871	15,780
55	78	105,391	6.57	98,558	1,708		1,119,832	15,780
56	79	109,607	6.83	102,500	1,777		1,077,415	15,780
57	80	113,991	7.11	106,600	1,848		1,028,069	15,780
58	81	118,551	7.39	110,864	1,922		971,202	15,780
59	82	123,293	7.69	115,299	1,999		906,181	15,780
60	83	128,225	7.99	119,911	2,078		832,327	15,780
61	84	133,354	8.31	124,707	2,162		748,914	15,780
62	85	138,688	8.65	129,696	2,248		655,161	15,780
63	86	144,235	8.99	134,883	2,338		550,235	15,780
64	87	150,005	9.35	140,279	2,431		433,245	15,780
65	88	156,005	9.73	145,890	2,529		303,235	15,780
66	89	162,245	10.12	151,725	2,630		159,184	15,780
67	90	168,735	10.52	157,794	2,735		0	15,780

6. In Spreadsheet 18.6, the real retirement annuity is $37,059.

   A 1% increase in the lower tax bracket will reduce the real retirement annuity to $36,815.

   A 1% increase in the highest tax bracket will reduce the real retirement annuity to $37,033.

   The increase in the highest tax bracket has a smaller impact because it applies to a small part of income.

7. The real retirement annuity in Spreadsheet 18.7 is $83,380.

   A decrease of 2% in the ROR will reduce the real retirement annuity to $50,900.

   An increase of 2% in the ROR will increase the real retirement annuity to $137,819.

   The percent reduction in the real annuity resulting from the decrease in ROR (39%) is much smaller than the percent increase resulting from the increase in ROR (65%). The reason the IRA shelter works as a hedge is that, if savings decline, then the marginal tax rate declines. The reverse is true when savings increase.

8. The real retirement annuity in Spreadsheet 18.8 is $ 49,153.

   A 1% increase in ROR will increase the real retirement annuity to $63,529.

   A 1% decrease in the rate of inflation will increase the real retirement annuity to $119,258.

   The reason inflation is more potent than ROR is that inflation affects the entire savings. Here, too, consumption during the labor years is fixed and hence the entire effect is transferred to the retirement annuity.

Spreadsheet 18.8: Adjusted for Change in ROR

	A	B	C	D	E	F	G	H
1	Retirement Years	Income growth	Rate of Inflation	Exemption now	Tax rates in	Saving rate	ROR	rROR
2	25	0.07	0.03	10000	Table 18.1	0.15	0.07	0.0388
3	Age	Income	Deflator	Exemption	Taxes	Savings	Cumulative Savings	rConsumption
4	30	50,000	1.00	10,000	8,000	6,300	6,300	35,700
5	31	53,500	1.03	10,300	8,640	6,793	13,534	36,958
9	35	70,128	1.16	11,593	11,764	9,370	54,231	42,262
19	45	137,952	1.56	15,580	28,922	19,707	298,059	57,333
29	55	271,372	2.09	20,938	64,661	41,143	987,189	79,076
39	65	533,829	2.81	28,139	145,999	92,460	2,827,329	104,970
40	Total			632,759	1,752,425	1,163,478	Real Annuity	63,529
41	RETIREMENT							
42	Age	Nom Withdraw	Deflator	Interest	Exemption	Taxes	Fund left	rConsumption
43	66	184,124	2.90	185,024	28,983	0	2,841,119	63,529
47	70	207,233	3.26	185,215	32,620	0	2,845,645	63,529
52	75	240,240	3.78	175,076	37,816	0	2,692,973	63,529
57	80	278,504	4.38	147,365	43,839	0	2,272,075	63,529
62	85	322,862	5.08	92,861	50,821	0	1,442,043	63,529
67	90	374,286	5.89	-1,714	58,916	0	0	63,529
68	Total			3,415,782		0		

Spreadsheet 18.8: Adjusted for Change in ROR

	A	B	C	D	E	F	G	H
1	Retirement Years	Income growth	Rate of Inflation	Exemption now	Tax rates in	Saving rate	ROR	rROR
2	25	0.07	0.02	10000	Table 18.1	0.15	0.06	0.0392
3	Age	Income	Deflator	Exemption	Taxes	Savings	Cumulative Savings	rConsumption
4	30	50,000	1.00	10,000	8,000	6,300	6,300	35,700
5	31	53,500	1.02	10,200	8,660	7,143	13,821	36,958
9	35	70,128	1.10	11,041	12,206	11,261	59,264	42,262
19	45	137,952	1.35	13,459	30,619	30,170	362,197	57,333
29	55	271,372	1.64	16,406	69,174	72,466	1,293,122	79,076
39	65	533,829	2.00	19,999	165,534	158,367	3,756,978	104,970
40	Total			519,944	1,929,174	1,901,289	Real Annuity	119,258
41	RETIREMENT							
42	Age	Nom Withdraw	Deflator	Interest	Exemption	Taxes	Fund left	rConsumption
43	66	243,272	2.04	210,822	20,399	0	3,739,125	119,258
47	70	263,325	2.21	203,087	22,080	0	3,603,662	119,258
52	75	290,733	2.44	182,991	24,379	0	3,250,278	119,258
57	80	320,992	2.69	146,857	26,916	0	2,613,730	119,258
62	85	354,401	2.97	88,299	29,717	0	1,581,215	119,258
67	90	391,288	3.28	-1,329	32,810	0	0	119,258
68	Total			3,567,574		0		

8. When deferring taxes to the last year of retirement, you must set money aside every
    year in order to accumulate a fund sufficient to pay the capital gains tax in a lump
    sum. To leave consumption fixed in real terms, a fixed real amount is set aside
    each year. We calculate the cumulative capital gains in cells D43 through D67.
    The nominal capital gains tax due in the final year appears in cell F68, and its real
    value is computed in cell B71. The real annuity required in order to pay the tax in
    cell B71 is shown in cells I43 through I67. The real amounts set aside in cells I43
    through I67 are deducted from real consumption.

    With annual payments of capital gains taxes (Spreadsheet 18.9), real consumption
    starts at $49,153 and ends at $46,358. When taxes are deferred to the last year of
    retirement, real consumption is fixed at the lower figure of $46,207. Thus, the
    progressivity of the tax code makes this option inferior.

Spreadsheet 18.9 Adjusted for a lump sum capital gains tax

	A	B	C	D	E	F	G	H	I	Q
1	Retirement Years	Income growth	Rate of Inflation	Exemption now	Tax rates in	Saving rate	ROR	rROR		
2	**25**	**0.07**	**0.03**	**10000**	**Table 18.1**	**0.15**	**0.06**	**0.0291**		
3	Age	Income	Deflator	Exemption	Taxes	Savings	Cumulative Savings	rConsumption		
4	30	50,000	1.00	10,000	8,000	6,300	6,300	35,700		
5	31	53,500	1.03	10,300	8,640	6,793	13,471	36,958		
9	35	70,128	1.16	11,593	11,764	9,370	52,995	42,262		
19	45	137,952	1.56	15,580	28,922	19,707	278,528	57,333		
29	55	271,372	2.09	20,938	64,661	41,143	883,393	79,076		
39	65	533,829	2.81	28,139	145,999	92,460	2,432,049	104,970		
40	**Total**				**1,752,425**	**1,163,478**	**Real Annuity**	**49,153**		
41	**RETIREMENT**				Tax rate on capital gain		**0.08**	**0.2**		
42	Age	Nom Withdraw	Deflator	Cum cap gains	Exemption	Taxes	Fund left	rConsumption	Savings*	Adj. rConsumption
43	66	142,460	2.90	1,414,494	28,983	0	2,435,512	49,153	2946	46,207
44	67	146,734	2.99	1,560,625	29,852	0	2,434,908	49,153	2946	46,207
45	68	151,136	3.07	1,706,719	30,748	0	2,429,867	49,153	2946	46,207
46	69	155,670	3.17	1,852,511	31,670	0	2,419,988	49,153	2946	46,207
47	70	160,340	3.26	1,997,710	32,620	0	2,404,847	49,153	2946	46,207
52	75	185,879	3.78	2,702,767	37,816	0	2,233,096	49,153	2946	46,207
57	80	215,484	4.38	3,332,479	43,839	0	1,846,348	49,153	2946	46,207
62	85	249,805	5.08	3,811,381	50,821	0	1,146,895	49,153	2946	46,207
63	86	257,299	5.23	3,880,195	52,346	0	958,409	49,153	2946	46,207
64	87	265,018	5.39	3,937,700	53,917	0	750,895	49,153	2946	46,207
65	88	272,969	5.55	3,982,753	55,534	0	522,980	49,153	2946	46,207
66	89	281,158	5.72	4,014,132	57,200	0	273,201	49,153	2946	46,207
67	90	289,593	5.89	4,030,524	58,916	952,371	0	-112,495	2946	46,207
68	**Total**				**1,056,691**	**952,371**				
69										
70	*Savings needed to pay taxes at end of retirement period (in real terms)									
71	*real taxes =	161,649								

10. Answers will vary.

11. The present value of labor income is $ 2,010,917 (at the rate of the applicable ROR). The present value of college tuition is $167,741. This is equal to: ($167,741/$2,010,917) = 8.34% of the present value of labor income. When college tuition increases by 1%, to $40,400, the present value of college tuition increases to $169,419, which is equal to 8.42% of labor income. Note that the present value of college tuition for two children makes up almost 10% of the present value of the entire household lifetime income.

12. Answers will vary.

13. The major traits are the degree of risk aversion and the bequest motive.

14. Answers will vary.

CHAPTER 19: TECHNICAL ANALYSIS

1.

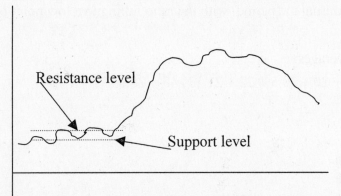

The resistance level is established by the history of the market reaching but failing to rise above a given price range. The support level is established by the history of the market reaching but failing to fall below a given price range.

2. $$\text{Trin} = \frac{\text{Volume declining} / \text{Number declining}}{\text{Volume advancing} / \text{Number advancing}} = \frac{582,866/1,488}{712,318/1,606} = 0.833$$

This trin ratio, which is below 1.0, would be taken as a bullish signal.

3.   Breadth:

Day	Advances	Declines	Net Advances	Cumulative Breadth
Thursday	1,736	1,394	342	+342
Friday	1,606	1,488	118	+460

Breadth is positive and increasing. This is a bullish signal (although no one would actually use a two-day measure as in this example).

4.   This exercise is left to the student.

5.   The confidence index increases from (8%/9%) = 0.889 to (9%/10%) = 0.900. This indicates slightly higher confidence. But the real reason for the increase in the index is the expectation of higher inflation, not higher confidence about the economy.

6.   September 17: market is down from previous days, trading volume is lower; thus, signal is bullish.

November 5: market is up, trading volume is lower; signal is bearish.

January 7: market is up, trading volume is down slightly from previous days, but still high; signal is bullish.

7. At the beginning of the period, the price of Computers, Inc. divided by the industry index was 0.39; by the end of the period, the ratio had increased to 0.50. As the ratio increased over the period, it appears that Computers, Inc. outperformed other firms in its industry. The overall trend, therefore, indicates relative strength, although some fluctuation existed during the period, with the ratio falling to a low point of 0.33.

8. Five day moving averages:

Days 1 – 5: (19.63 + 20 + 20.5 + 22 + 21.13) / 5 = 20.65
Days 2 – 6 = 21.13
Days 3 – 7 = 21.50
Days 4 – 8 = 21.90
Days 5 – 9 = 22.13
Days 6 – 10 = 22.68
Days 7 – 11 = 23.18
Days 8 – 12 = 23.45   ← Buy signal (day 12 price > moving average)
Days 9 – 13 = 23.38
Days 10 – 14 = 23.15
Days 11 – 15 = 22.50
Days 12 – 16 = 21.65
Days 13 – 17 = 20.95
Days 14 – 18 = 20.28
Days 15 – 19 = 19.38
Days 16 – 20 = 19.05
Days 17 – 21 = 18.93   ← Sell signal (day 21 price < moving average)
Days 18 – 22 = 19.28
Days 19 – 23 = 19.93
Days 20 – 24 = 21.05
Days 21 – 25 = 22.05
Days 22 – 26 = 23.18
Days 23 – 27 = 24.13
Days 24 – 28 = 25.13
Days 25 – 29 = 26.00
Days 26 – 30 = 26.80
Days 27 – 31 = 27.45
Days 28 – 32 = 27.80
Days 29 – 33 = 27.90   ← Buy signal (day 33 price > moving average)
Days 30 – 34 = 28.20
Days 31 – 35 = 28.45
Days 32 – 36 = 28.65
Days 33 – 37 = 29.05
Days 34 – 38 = 29.25
Days 35 – 39 = 29.00
Days 36 – 40 = 28.75

9.

Price					
30				X	
28				X	0
26				X	0
24		X		X	
22		X	0	X	
20		X	0	X	
18			0	X	
16			0		

Buy (arrow pointing to X in column at price ~26)

Sell (arrow pointing to 0 at price ~18)

A sell signal occurs at a price of approximately $19, which is similar to a sell signal derived from the moving average rule. However, the buy signals are not the same.

10. This pattern shows a lack of breadth. Even though the index is up, more stocks declined than advanced, which indicates a "lack of broad-based support" for the rise in the index.

11.

Day	Advances	Declines	Net Advances	Cumulative Breadth
1	906	704	202	202
2	653	986	-333	-131
3	721	789	- 68	-199
4	503	968	-465	-664
5	497	1,095	-598	-1,262
6	970	702	268	-994
7	1,002	609	393	-601
8	903	722	181	-420
9	850	748	102	-318
10	766	766	0	-318

The signal is bearish as cumulative breadth is negative; however, the negative number is declining in magnitude, indicative of improvement. Perhaps the worst of the bear market has passed.

12. $$\text{Trin} = \frac{\text{Volume declining/Number declining}}{\text{Volume advancing/Number advancing}} = \frac{240 \text{ million} / 704}{330 \text{ million} / 906} = 0.936$$

This is a slightly bullish indicator, with average volume in advancing issues a bit greater than average volume in declining issues.

13. Confidence Index = $\dfrac{\text{Yield on top - rated corporate bonds}}{\text{Yield on intermediate - grade corporate bonds}}$

This year: Confidence Index = (8%/9%) = 0.889

Last year: Confidence Index = (9%/10%) = 0.900

Thus, the confidence index is decreasing.

CHAPTER 20: PERFORMANCE EVALUATION
AND ACTIVE PORTFOLIO MANAGEMENT

1. d.

2. c.

3. b.

4. a.

	E(r)	σ	β
Stock A	11%	10%	0.8
Stock B	14%	31%	1.5
Market index	12%	20%	1.0
Risk-free asset	6%	0%	0.0

    The alphas for the two stocks are:

    $$\alpha_A = 11\% - [6\% + 0.8(12\% - 6\%)] = 0.2\%$$

    $$\alpha_B = 14\% - [6\% + 1.5(12\% - 6\%)] = -1.0\%$$

    Ideally, you would want to take a long position in Stock A and a short position in Stock B.

    b. If you hold only one of the two stocks, then the Sharpe measure is the appropriate criterion:

    $$S_A = \frac{11-6}{10} = 0.5$$

    $$S_B = \frac{14-6}{31} = 0.26$$

    Therefore, using the Sharpe criterion, Stock A is preferred.

5. We first distinguish between timing ability and selection ability. The intercept of the scatter diagram is a measure of stock selection ability. If the manager tends to have a positive excess return even when the market's performance is merely "neutral" (i.e., the market has zero excess return) then we conclude that the manager has, on average, made good stock picks. In other words, stock selection must be the source of the positive excess returns.

    Timing ability is indicated by the curvature of the plotted line. Lines that become steeper as you move to the right of the graph show good timing ability. The steeper slope shows that the manager maintained higher portfolio sensitivity to market swings (i.e., a higher beta) in periods when the market performed well. This ability to choose more market-sensitive securities in anticipation of market upturns is the essence of good timing. In contrast, a declining slope as you move to the right indicates that the portfolio was more sensitive to the market when the market performed poorly, and less sensitive to the market when the market performed well. This indicates poor timing.

We can therefore classify performance ability for the four managers as follows:

	Selection Ability	Timing Ability
A	Bad	Good
B	Good	Good
C	Good	Bad
D	Bad	Bad

6.   a.   Actual: $(0.70 \times 2.0\%) + (0.20 \times 1.0\%) + (0.10 \times 0.5\%) = 1.65\%$

          Bogey: $(0.60 \times 2.5\%) + (0.30 \times 1.2\%) + (0.10 \times 0.5\%) = 1.91\%$

          *Under*performance $= 1.91\% - 1.65\% = 0.26\%$

  b.   *Security Selection:*

Market	Portfolio Performance	Index Performance	Excess Performance	Manager's Portfolio Weight	Contribution
Equity	2.0%	2.5%	-0.5%	0.70	-0.35%
Bonds	1.0%	1.2%	-0.2%	0.20	-0.04%
Cash	0.5%	0.5%	0.0%	0.10	0.00%
			Contribution of security selection:		-0.39%

  c.   *Asset Allocation:*

Market	Actual Weight	Benchmark Weight	Excess Weight	Index Return minus Bogey	Contribution
Equity	0.70	0.60	0.10	0.59%	0.059%
Bonds	0.20	0.30	-0.10	-0.71%	0.071%
Cash	0.10	0.10	0.00	-1.41%	0.000%
			Contribution of asset allocation:		0.130%

       Summary

Security selection	-0.39%
Asset allocation	0.13%
Excess performance	-0.26%

7.   Support: A manager could be a better forecaster in one scenario than another. For example, a high-beta manager will do better in up markets and worse in down markets. Therefore, we should observe performance over an entire cycle. Also, to the extent that observing a manager over an entire cycle increases the number of observations, it would improve the reliability of the measurement.

      Contradict: If we adequately control for exposure to the market (i.e., adjust for beta), then market performance should not affect the relative performance of individual managers. It is therefore not necessary to wait for an entire market cycle to pass before you evaluate a manager.

8.	It does, to some degree. If those manager groups are sufficiently homogeneous with respect to style, then relative performance is a decent benchmark. However, one would like to be able to adjust for the additional variation in style or risk choice that remains among managers in any comparison group. In addition, investors might prefer an "investable" alternative such as a passive index to which they can compare a manager's performance. After all, passive investors do not have the choice of investing in "the median manager," since the identity of that manager is not known until *after* the investment period.

9.	The manager's alpha is: $10\% - [6\% + 0.5(14\% - 6\%-)] = 0$

10.	a.	$\alpha_A = 24\% - [12\% + 1.0(21\% - 12\%)] = 3.0\%$

$\alpha_B = 30\% - [12\% + 1.5(21\% - 12\%)] = 4.5\%$

$T_A = (24 - 12)/1 = 12$

$T_B = (30 - 12)/1.5 = 12$

As an addition to a passive diversified portfolio, both A and B are candidates because they both have positive alphas.

b.	(i)	The managers may have been trying to time the market. In that case, the SCL of the portfolios may be non-linear.

(ii)	One year of data is too small a sample.

(iii)	The portfolios may have significantly different levels of diversification. If both have the same risk-adjusted return, the less diversified portfolio has a higher exposure to risk because of its higher diversifiable risk. Since the above measure adjusts for systematic risk only, it does not tell the entire story.

11.	a.	Indeed, the one year results were terrible, but one year is a poor statistical base from which to draw inferences. Moreover, the fund manager was directed to adopt a long-term horizon. The Board specifically instructed the investment manager to give priority to long term results.

b.	The sample of pension funds held a much larger share in equities compared to the Alpine pension fund. The stock and bond indexes indicate that equity returns significantly exceeded bond returns. The Alpine fund manager was explicitly directed to hold down risk, investing at most 25% of fund assets in common stocks. (Alpine's beta was also somewhat defensive). Alpine should not be held responsible for an asset allocation policy dictated by the client.

c.	Over the five-year period, Alpine's alpha, which measures risk-adjusted performance compared to the market, was positive:

$\alpha = 13.3\% - [7.5\% + 0.9(13.8\% - 7.5\%)] = 0.13\%$

d.   Note that, over the last five years, and particularly the last one year, bond performance has been poor; this is significant because this is the asset class that Alpine had been encouraged to hold. Within this asset class, however, the Alpine fund fared much better than the index, as shown in the last two lines of the table. Moreover, despite the fact that the bond index underperformed both the actuarial return and T-bills, the Alpine fund outperformed both for the five-year period. On a risk-adjusted basis, Alpine's performance *within* each asset class has been superior. The overall disappointing returns were the result of the heavy asset allocation weighting towards bonds, which was the Board's, not the fund manager's, choice.

e.   A trustee may not care about the time-weighted return, but that return is more indicative of the manager's performance. After all, the manager has no control over the cash inflow to the fund.

12.   See the Black-Scholes formula in Chapter 15. Substitute:
Current stock price = S_0 = $1.0
Exercise price = X = $(1 + r_f)$ = 1.01
Standard deviation = σ = 0.055
Risk-free interest rate = r_f = 0.01
Time to maturity of option = T = 1
Recall that $\ln(1 + y)$ is approximately equal to y, for small y, and that $N(-x) = [1 - N(x)]$. Then the value of a call option on $1 of the equity portfolio, with exercise price X = $(1 + r_f)$, is:

$$C = 2N(\sigma/2) - 1$$

$N(\sigma/2)$ is the cumulative standard normal density for the value of half the standard deviation of the equity portfolio.

$$C = 2N(.0275) - 1$$

Interpolating from the standard normal table (Table 15.2):

$$C = 2[0.5080 + 0.75(0.5120 - 0.5080)] - 1 = 0.0220 = 2.2\%$$

Hence the added value of a perfect timing strategy is 2.2% per month.

13.   a.   Using the relative frequencies to estimate the conditional probabilities P_1 and P_2 for timers A and B, we find:

	Timer A	Timer B
P_1	78/135 = 0.58	86/135 = 0.64
P_2	57/92 = 0.62	50/92 = 0.54
$P^* = P_1 + P_2 - 1$	0.20	0.18

The data suggest that timer A is the better forecaster.

b.   Using the following equation to value the imperfect timing services of Timer A and Timer B:

$$C(P^*) = C(P_1 + P_2 - 1)$$

$$C_A(P^*) = 2.2\% \times 0.20 = 0.44\% \text{ per month}$$

$$C_B(P^*) = 2.2\% \times 0.18 = 0.40\% \text{ per month}$$

Timer B's added value is greater by 4 basis points per month.

14.   a.

Alpha (α)	Expected excess return
$\alpha_i = r_i - [r_f + \beta_i(r_M - r_f)]$	$E(r_i) - r_f$
$\alpha_A = 20\% - [8\% + 1.3(16\% - 8\%)] = 1.6\%$	$20\% - 8\% = 12\%$
$\alpha_B = 18\% - [8\% + 1.8(16\% - 8\%)] = -4.4\%$	$18\% - 8\% = 10\%$
$\alpha_C = 17\% - [8\% + 0.7(16\% - 8\%)] = 3.4\%$	$17\% - 8\% = 9\%$
$\alpha_D = 12\% - [8\% + 1.0(16\% - 8\%)] = -4.0\%$	$12\% - 8\% = 4\%$

Stocks A and C have positive alphas, whereas stocks B and D have negative alphas.

The residual variances are:

$$\sigma^2(e_A) = 58^2 = 3364$$

$$\sigma^2(e_B) = 71^2 = 5041$$

$$\sigma^2(e_C) = 60^2 = 3600$$

$$\sigma^2(e_D) = 55^2 = 3025$$

b.   To construct the optimal risky portfolio, we first determine the optimal active portfolio. Using the Treynor-Black technique, we construct the active portfolio:

	$\dfrac{\alpha}{\sigma^2(e)}$	$\dfrac{\alpha / \sigma^2(e)}{\Sigma \alpha / \sigma^2(e)}$
A	.000476	−0.6142
B	−.000873	1.1265
C	.000944	−1.2181
D	−.001322	1.7058
Total	−.000775	1.0000

Do not be disturbed by the fact that the positive alpha stocks get negative weights and vice versa. The entire position in the active portfolio will turn out to be negative, returning everything to good order.

With these weights, the forecast for the active portfolio is:

$$\alpha = [-0.6142 \times 1.6] + [1.1265 \times (-4.4)] - [1.2181 \times 3.4] + [1.7058 \times (-4.0)]$$
$$= -16.90\%$$

$$\beta = [-0.6142 \times 1.3] + [1.1265 \times 1.8] - [1.2181 \times 0.70] + [1.7058 \times 1] = 2.08$$

The high beta (higher than any individual beta) results from the short positions in the relatively low beta stocks and the long positions in the relatively high beta stocks.

$$\sigma^2(e) = [(-0.6142)^2 \times 3364] + [1.1265^2 \times 5041] + [(-1.2181)^2 \times 3600] + [1.7058^2 \times 3025]$$
$$= 21809.6$$

$$\sigma(e) = 147.68\%$$

Here, again, the levered position in stock B [with the high $\sigma^2(e)$] overcomes the diversification effect, and results in a high residual standard deviation.

The optimal risky portfolio has a proportion w^* in the active portfolio, computed as follows:

$$w_0 = \frac{\alpha/\sigma^2(e)}{[E(r_M)-r_f]/\sigma_M^2} = \frac{-16.90/21809.6}{8/23^2} = -0.05124$$

The negative position is justified for the reason given earlier.

The adjustment for beta is:

$$w^* = \frac{w_0}{1+(1-\beta)w_0} = \frac{-0.05124}{1+(1-2.08)(-0.05124)} = -0.0486$$

Because w* is negative, we end up with a positive position in stocks with positive alphas and vice versa. The position in the index portfolio is:

$$1 - (-0.0486) = 1.0486$$

c. To calculate Sharpe's measure for the optimal risky portfolio we compute the appraisal ratio for the active portfolio and Sharpe's measure for the market portfolio. The appraisal ratio of the *active portfolio* is:

$$A = \alpha/\sigma(e) = -16.90/147.68 = -0.1144$$
$$A^2 = 0.0131$$

Hence, the square of Sharpe's measure (S) of the *optimized risky portfolio* is:

$$S^2 = S_M^2 + A^2 = \left(\frac{8}{23}\right)^2 + 0.0131 = 0.1341$$

$$S = 0.3662$$

Compare this to the market's Sharpe measure:

$S_M = 8/23 = 0.3478$

The difference is 0.0184.

Note that the only-moderate improvement in performance results from the fact that only a small position is taken in the active portfolio A because of its large residual variance.

We calculate the "Modigliani-squared" (M^2) measure, as follows:

$E(r_{P*}) = r_f + S_P \, \sigma_{M'} = 8\% + (0.3662 \times 23\%) = 16.423\%$

$M^2 = E(r_{P*}) - E(r_M) = 16.423\% - 16\% = 0.423\%$

CHAPTER 21: INTERNATIONAL INVESTING

1. a. $10,000/2 = £5,000

    £5,000/£40 = 125 shares

    b.   To fill in the table, we use the relation:

$$1 + r(US) = [(1 + r_f(UK)]\frac{E_1}{E_0}$$

Price per Share (£)	Pound-Denominated Return (%)	Dollar-Denominated Return (%) for Year-End Exchange Rate		
		$1.80/£	$2.00/£	$2.20/£
£35	-12.5%	-21.25%	-12.5%	-3.75%
£40	0.0%	-10.00%	0.0%	10.00%
£45	12.5%	1.25%	12.5%	23.75%

    c.   The dollar-denominated return equals the pound-denominated return when the exchange rate is unchanged over the year.

2.   The standard deviation of the pound-denominated return (using 3 degrees of freedom) is 10.21%. The dollar-denominated return has a standard deviation of 13.10% (using 9 degrees of freedom), greater than the pound-denominated standard deviation. This is due to the addition of exchange rate risk.

3.   First we calculate the dollar value of the 125 shares of stock in each scenario. Then we add the profits from the forward contract in each scenario.

Price per Share (£)	Exchange Rate:	Dollar Value of Stock at Given Exchange Rate		
		$1.80/£	$2.00/£	$2.20/£
£35		7,875	8,750	9,625
£40		9,000	10,000	11,000
£45		10,125	11,250	12,375
Profits on Forward Exchange: $[= 5000(2.10 - E_1)]$		1,500	500	-500

Price per Share (£)	Exchange Rate:	Total Dollar Proceeds at Given Exchange Rate		
		$1.80/£	$2.00/£	$2.20/£
£35		9,375	9,250	9,125
£40		10,500	10,500	10,500
£45		11,625	11,750	11,875

Finally, calculate the dollar-denominated rate of return, recalling that the initial investment was $10,000:

Price per		Rate of return (%) at Given Exchange Rate		
Share (£)	Exchange Rate:	$1.80/£	$2.00/£	$2.20/£
£35		-6.25%	-7.50%	-8.75%
£40		5.00%	5.00%	5.00%
£45		16.25%	17.50%	18.75%

   b.   The standard deviation is now 10.24%. This is lower than the unhedged dollar-denominated standard deviation, and is only slightly higher than the standard deviation of the pound-denominated return.

4.   **Currency Selection**

EAFE: $[0.30 \times (-10\%)] + (0.10 \times 0\%) + (0.60 \times 10\%) = 3.0\%$

Manager: $[0.35 \times (-10\%)] + (0.15 \times 0\%) + (0.50 \times 10\%) = 1.5\%$

Loss of 1.5% relative to EAFE.

Country Selection

EAFE: $(0.30 \times 20\%) + (0.10 \times 15\%) + (0.60 \times 25\%) = 22.50\%$

Manager: $(0.35 \times 20\%) + (0.15 \times 15\%) + (0.50 \times 25\%) = 21.75\%$

Loss of 0.75% relative to EAFE.

Stock Selection

$[(18\% - 20\%) \times 0.35] + [(20\% - 15\%) \times 0.15] + [(20\% - 25\%) \times 0.50] = -2.45\%$

Loss of 2.45% relative to EAFE.

5. $1 + r(US) = [1 + r_f(UK)] \times (F_0/E_0) = 1.08 \times (1.85/1.75) = 1.1417 \Rightarrow r(US) = 14.17\%$

6.   You can now purchase ($10,000/$1.75) = £5,714.29, which will grow with 8% interest to £6,171.43. Therefore, to lock in your return, you need to sell forward £6,171.43 at the forward exchange rate.

7.   a.   We exchange $1 million for foreign currency at the current exchange rate and sell forward the amount of foreign currency we will accumulate 90 days from now. For the yen investment, we initially receive:

      1 million × 133.05 = ¥133.05 million

    Invest for 90 days to accumulate:

      ¥133.05 × [1 + (0.076/4)] = ¥135.57795 million.

    (We divide the quoted 90-day rate by 4, since quoted money market interest rates typically are annualized using simple interest and assuming a 360-day year.)

If we sell this number of yen forward at the forward exchange rate of ¥133.47/dollar, we will end up with:

$$\frac{135.57795 \text{million}}{133.47} = \$1.015793 \text{ million}$$

The 90-day dollar interest rate is 1.5793%.

Similarly, the dollar proceeds from the 90-day Swiss franc investment will be:

$$[\$1 \text{ million} \times 1.526] \times \frac{1+(.086/4)}{1.5348} = \$1.015643 \text{ million}$$

The 90-day dollar interest rate is 1.5643%, almost the same as that in the yen investment.

b.   The nearly identical results in either currency are expected and reflect the interest-rate parity relationship. This example thus asserts that the pricing relationships between interest rates and spot and forward exchange rates must make covered investments in any currency equally attractive.

c.   The dollar-hedged rate of return on default-free government securities in Japan is 1.5793% and in Switzerland is 1.5643%. Therefore, the 90-day interest rate available on U.S. government securities must be between 1.5643% and 1.5793%. This corresponds to an annual rate between 6.2572% and 6.3172%, which is less than the APR in Japan or Switzerland. (For consistency with our earlier calculations, we annualize the 90-day rate using the convention of the money market, assuming a 360-day year and simple interest). The lower interest rate in the U.S. makes sense, as the relationship between forward and spot exchange rates indicates that the U.S. dollar is expected to appreciate against both the Japanese yen and the Swiss franc.

8.   The relationship between the spot and forward exchange rates indicates that the U.S. dollar is expected to appreciate against the Swiss franc. Therefore, the interest rate in the U.S. is higher, in order to induce investors to invest in the U.S.

9.   a.   Using the relationship:

$$F_0 = E_0 \times \frac{1+r_f(US)}{1+r_f(UK)} = 1.50 \times \frac{1.05}{1.07} = 1.472$$

b. If the forward rate is 1.49 dollars per pound, then the forward rate is overpriced. To create an arbitrage profit, use the following strategy:

Action	Initial Cash Flow	Cash Flow at Time T
Enter a contract to sell £1.07 at a (futures price) of $F_0 = \$1.49$	0.0	$1.07 \times (1.49 - E_1)$
Borrow $1.50 in the U.S.	1.50	-1.50×1.05
Convert the borrowed dollars to pounds, and lend in the U.K. at a 7% interest rate	-1.50	$1.07 \times E_1$
Total	0	0.0193

10. a. Lend in the U.K.

   b. Borrow in the U.S.

   c. According to the interest rate parity relationship, the forward rate should be:

$$F_0 = E_0 \times \frac{1 + r_f(US)}{1 + r_f(UK)} = 2.00 \times \frac{1.05}{1.07} = 1.9626$$

The strategy will involve:

Action	Initial Cash Flow	Cash Flow at Time T
Enter a contract to sell £1.07 at a (futures price) of $F_0 = \$1.97$	0.0	$1.07 \times (1.97 - E_1)$
Borrow $2.00 in the U.S.	2.00	-2.00×1.05
Convert the borrowed dollars to pounds, and lend in the U.K. at a 7% interest rate	-2.00	$1.07 \times E_1$
Total	0	0.0079

11. a. The primary rationale is the opportunity for diversification. Factors that contribute to low correlations of stock returns across national boundaries are:
   i.   imperfect correlation of business cycles
   ii.   imperfect correlation of interest rates
   iii. imperfect correlation of inflation rates
   iv.   exchange rate volatility

b. Obstacles to international investing are:

    i. <u>Availability of information</u>, including insufficient data on which to base investment decisions. Interpreting and evaluating data that is different in form and/or content than the routinely available and widely understood U.S. data is difficult. Also, much foreign data is reported with a considerable lag.

    ii. <u>Liquidity</u>, in terms of the ability to buy or sell, in size and in a timely manner, without affecting the market price. Most foreign exchanges offer (relative to U.S. norms) limited trading, and experience greater price volatility. Moreover, only a (relatively) small number of individual foreign stocks enjoy liquidity comparable to that in the U.S., although this situation is improving steadily.

    iii. <u>Transaction costs</u>, particularly when viewed as a combination of commission plus spread plus market impact costs, are well above U.S. levels in most foreign markets. This, of course, adversely affects return realization.

    iv. <u>Political risk</u>.

    v. <u>Foreign currency risk</u>, although to a great extent, this can be hedged.

c. The asset-class performance data for this particular period reveal that non-U.S. dollar bonds provided a small incremental return advantage over U.S. dollar bonds, but at a considerably higher level of risk. Each category of fixed income assets outperformed the S&P 500 Index measure of U.S. equity results with regard to both risk and return, which is certainly an unexpected outcome. Within the equity area, non-U.S. stocks, represented by the EAFE Index, outperformed U.S. stocks by a considerable margin with only slightly more risk. In contrast to U.S. equities, this asset category performed as it should relative to fixed income assets, providing more return for the higher risk involved.

Concerning the Account Performance Index, its position on the graph reveals an aggregate outcome that is superior to the sum of its component parts. To some extent, this is due to the beneficial effect on performance resulting from multi-market diversification and the differential covariances involved. In this case, the portfolio manager(s) (apparently) achieved an on-balance positive alpha, adding to total portfolio return by their actions. The addition of international (i.e., non-U.S.) securities to a portfolio that would otherwise have held only domestic (U.S.) securities clearly worked to the advantage of this fund over this time period.